TICKET TO ALL-INCLUSIVE LIFE

Your Life-Changing Guidebook

ANI SHAHVERDYAN

Ticket to All-Inclusive Life

www.anishahverdyan.com

This book is dedicated to Mr. Garik Shahverdyan, my lovely husband who has always believed in me and encouraged me on my way to success.
Thank you for your unconditional love and trust.

CONTENT

INTRODUCTION

My dear reader,

First off, I want to congratulate you on starting to read this book. Your willingness to go through it displays readiness to make your life wonderful by achieving greatness in all aspects of it.

The book you are reading now is the outcome of thorough analysis of my personal life and the lives of people whom I have ever met. It is the service I render to this planet, my way of expressing gratitude to the Universe for being exceedingly generous to me by guiding and responding and opening her sacred truths.

This book reveals the empirical rules of notching up spectacular success in life. Success of itself has a broad definition, hence there is a great deal of know-hows to achieve it. In this book, I have combined all the methods and approaches of achieving success in every aspect of life because, at the end of the day, all we want is an all-inclusive life.

I want to emphasize that the rules were not invented by me. Moreover, they have been accessible to humanity since day one and their actuality is undeniable up till now. My master plan was to locate and incorporate them into a single book of success. People who seek positive changes in life, will find ideal formulas which will guide them through the journey of all-round success.

It took me several years to finalize it. The nub of the matter is, I wanted to make sure the rules I unearthed are deadly accurate and personally practiced. And last but not least, I needed to see vivid results in my own life right before introducing them to you. Since you are reading this book, I am the concrete proof of those universal rules that have a profound impact on every single human being. If properly used, these principles and formulas can literally bring long-lasting happiness which is so desperately sought by humans.

It`s so depressive for me to see people failing to find these simple, yet unnoticeable basics and sometimes even wrecking their lives on the way. My dearest wish is to see that everyone knows how to realize their dreams, achieve success and feel satisfied with their own lives. Therefore, I pray that this book will guide you on your way to success and prosperity. I do believe once the ideas accentuated here spread out globally, we will all have access to an all-inclusive life, and the world will become a way better place.

Prior to expanding upon the essence of the book, I want you to know that we all have an unlimited amount of chances and ultimate potential to make our lives outstandingly magnificent.

It may sound cliché that everyone has the ability of achieving notable success if only they are willing to make it happen, but I dare to say that this book is going to prove that statement to you.

ALLEGORY ABOUT SUCCESS AND FAILURE

There are two major poles which heavily influence people—the pole of Success and the pole of Failure. Those poles have their own gravity, i.e. magnetic influence on us, they are equally powerful, and both try to get the most of us. In fact, we are born in the middle of those two poles—right on the equator. At an early stage of our life, we mainly depend on other people, including parents and relatives. The latter take us on their trip either to the pole of Success or to the pole of Failure. As newbies we don`t realize the location they are directing us to. We can't even change it until we grow up and become aware about the existence of the poles, i.e. wise enough to look at our own compass. This is what happens next:

- people either live their life in an autopilot mode eventually ending up in the pole of Failure,
- people become aware of the two poles and start moving their direction to the pole of Success.

How does it happen? The first group of people are ignorant of the definition of success and failure; they usually live without realizing the existence of the two poles. The impulses of Success and Failure bring them neither triumph nor pain as they don`t recognize them clearly. Their lifestyle reminds an abandoned ship with no captain abroad. Consequently, blustery winds decide their direction. Once sailing to the black waters, the frenzied attacks by Failure become more and more frequent. In the aftermath, they start feeling oppressed and gradually lose their vital energy. Being blind about the causes of their troubles they don`t even know what to resist and eventually they end up in the center of Failure—the place from where Success is not even seen on the horizon.

The second group of people learn about the existence of the two poles as time elapses. They study their nature and keep their compass at hand from the word go. They know where they are sailing and are not even half afraid of the vicious attacks by Failure. They keep on navigating with billowing sails to Success instead of resting in the waters of Failure. In fact, it doesn`t really matter how astray they were before the very enlightenment which propelled them into realizing the direction they were heading to. Surprisingly, the center of the pole of Failure doesn`t have a forcing power to keep people penned up if they are not willing to stay. Nothing is stronger than resolute people with determined mind and concentrated actions. This group of people get overly galvanized by the first impulses of Success. Success keeps them going faster with confidence and finally they reach the heart of Success!

CHAPTER 1

WHO ARE YOU?

I looked into the mirror of souls and said,
"Nice to meet me."

Who are you? In actual fact, this question relates neither to your life story, nor your descent, not even age, job or educational background.

This question is addressed to you by yourself. **Who are YOU?** Ask yourself. What makes you feel yourself? Why are you here? How do you evince your existence? What feeds your soul and makes you happy? What forms the backbone of your life? What dreams do you cherish? What means success to you? What makes you look around with satisfaction and fulfillment of life?

By nature, every human being is inclined to imitate starting from our first days. People do this unconsciously and often get lost in the crowd as they resemble the behavioral features of others: their character, manners and even dreams! I am more than certain that every life has a unique purpose.

Life is gifted to us for the realization of our personal and exclusive potential. Basically, there are no useless people in the world. The reason behind the misconception is that the majority live without finding out their element—the place they are necessary the most. This is the primary reason they fail to recognize the real value of life. Every person must spend a while analyzing his own self to become capable of understanding his life`s purpose. Only this way one can learn to produce his true self.

I openly confess, answering the above-mentioned questions is way tougher than it may seem at first glance. These questions need an in-depth analysis of your own self so that you become able to arrive at correct answers. It took me several years to accumulate this wealth of experience.

Let me drop a tantalizing hint so that you can answer these questions easily; **the purpose of life is hidden in the reasons of our unconditional choices**. By finding the underlying reasons, you are digging into an unknown territory, an uncharted planet inside you, a depth where your unique strengths are hidden. Bear it in mind, that conducting an interview with the most paramount person in the world—yourself, is not as easy as falling off the log.

To crack these questions, I advise to recall the very beginning of your life; I tend to believe that our purest feelings were evoked when we were very young. Suffice it to say, we welcomed and cherished little joys back in the time when we were kids. We were blissfully ignorant about this world, yet we loved it so much... Maybe we knew something essential about life, something gifted to us by birth which we gradually stopped using and forgot? But, what did we forget? **That we were born with happiness already? Is inborn happiness the supreme way to enjoy the life?** I wonder if anyone fully grown still welcomes the first shines of the sun into his life after waking up early in the morning. I wonder if anyone still looks around with excitement as if he sees everything for the first time. I wonder if anyone can still smile without concealed reasons. I still wonder if anyone warmly greets life and lives as if it lasts only a day.

When born we had a sense of security, yet we didn't realize it. As we grew up we were lulled into thinking about our own ways of caring for ourselves and stumbled upon obstacles such as inferior education, lack of skills, problems related to hunting a well-paid job, odd jobs which hinder the development of our unique potential, drawbacks in building healthy family relationships, severe lack of time for personal growth, much-needed rest, meeting our friends on a regular basis, and with these obstacles surmounted, saving or winning back our precious health.

We clearly realize that making things work on our own is a much more complicated burden compared to the tasks we were loaded with as kids. As a matter of fact, we make major mistakes at this very period. To make things worse, the blindness about our mistakes paralyzes us and the incapability to solve our problems slowly turns our lives into a chaos. We stumble upon a failure after a failure as times goes by and eventually the enthusiasm which we had in the beginning gets vanished. This is the primary reason that we witness individuals with decent age doing jobs they hate with a sole purpose to make both ends meet. Barely keeping families and constantly complaining on the unfairness of life has become an indelible part of people`s life that erred unknowingly.

Please, stop reading for a short while and try to think about the questions addressed to you in the beginning of this paragraph. It`s critically important that you come up with your personal answers to them with your mind free from trials and tribulations of life. I heartily recommend thinking about the answers right before you drift into sleep; our imagination becomes brighter at bedtime as we become daring to give freedom to our dreams.

Apparently, there is not a single individual who failed to have dreams that are hard to recall yet hard to forget. Lost somewhere in the middle they wait for their rediscovery. Grant them a chance. Take a ticket to your dreamland full of opportunities which are on the mettle to be materialized. Just do it and you will return on your wings. It`s fine if you lose your sleep tonight because of these sobering thoughts. Each of us has had sleepless nights spent in vain, hence this mega purpose is unquestionably worth it. Your answers may not occur overnight or over a week, or even over a year. Yet, they will eventually emerge if you keep your endeavors on finding them.

The moment you reveal yourself you will grant freedom to your inner power reserves to come to light. Once you come to realize your deep recess, the things that feed your soul, the dreams your mind cherishes, you will immediately shift to the next question—**how can I animate my dreams?**

TURNING DREAMS INTO GOALS

We all have power,
but those controlling it are the truly powerful ones.

Dreams are a human product that mirror possible reality which is yet to come. They are the sinew of our achievements. Dreams are energized through our most valuable wishes, hopes and ambitions. Yet, turning them into goals and then into reality requires a precise blueprint. Once a dream is blueprinted, it is no longer just a dream but a goal, a project.

If you ask around, you will be astonished to learn that the overwhelming majority of people have dreams similar to yours. But as ill luck would have it, most people consider dreams a fantasy—something bright and scintillating and yet undefined, something pretty distant and unreachable that can be used only in present conditional tense. In point of facts, dreams which don`t have a vivid structure or a virtual body simply can't turn into a solid matter. As time goes by, they just fade into oblivion somewhere in the deep recess of our memories.

One can spot uncertain dreamers everywhere, what is even worse, there is a great number of people with chancy dreams. The latter don't have the slightest idea about their mission in this world—the mission to fulfill their dreams and live a beautiful life.

Our dreams are our orders beamed straight from the universe. They should be designated to have a name, a form and a body. If you have a dream, you need to

- think about it,
- visualize it,
- feel it through your senses,
- wish it with all your heart,
- treat it as a potential that will materialize as soon as you give it a momentum.

The story has thousands of names of prominent people, whose biographies strongly inspire us. In reality, their lives were not easier than the lives we live. They attained greatness not because they were destined to reach it. They attained greatness not through force of favorable circumstances. In fact, the only reason behind their bigness is that they had a vivid idea about what they wanted to get from life and took actions toward it.

The world we see nowadays mirrors the story of the bravest dreamers. They carved out a truly beautiful place for us to live. Formidable difficulties of today's world would probably look like a joke for people born less than a hundred years ago. Back in the past, people were fighting fiercely for staying alive and their freedom! Therefore, it can`t be understood that in our world full of abundance where the individuals and their inseparable rights are on the very spotlight, still there are people who prefer to adapt to misery and misfortune instead of transforming their dreams into reality.

Believe you me, I don't mean to underestimate anyone. My own life has been fraught with enormous obstacles from the very beginning. Conversely, the dire problems helped me work harder on my dreams, and today I stand strong having achieved a great many of my goals. Importantly, I do realize that **there is a way to succeed even from the point zero or somewhere below it.** Simple as that, you must make your dreams the hub of the universe and struggle until they become your reality. Don`t be afraid to get hurt during the battles which lead to victories. At the end of the day you will not be ashamed of your scars but will undoubtedly be proud of them; they will stigmatize the importance of your dreams to you. So, I strongly encourage you, **don`t just dream but dream out**; **let the outside world become the reflection of your dreams**. **Choose your destiny not by counting the obstacles but by hunting your dreams**. **Believe undoubtedly that you can jump higher than your height**. The taste of tomorrow depends on the seeds you plant today. So, work on your dreams, chase them the way your shadow chases you.

Just look around! Do you see that we all have the same ingredients for success? **24 hours a day and a freedom of choice**. So, figure out what to do with each of your own 24s to reach success!

THE ESSENCE OF SUCCESS AND FAILURE

Before we embark upon setting goals and achieving them, we better define what success and failure denote to us. It's beyond the bounds of possibility to recognize success and failure without being introduced to them.

Success is the capacity of changing something which will result in long-lasting joy and satisfaction.

The rules of success are as old as the world, yet very few are able to achieve it. Those rules are available to humanity like a well-served meal, however some of them require strong teeth. It`s worth mentioning that there are people who have been constantly looking for magical quick tricks for success in books or facile ways to attract success through luck. To them, I have to say, it is a wild goose chase and this book has nothing to do with it. Luck deals with lottery; the rest of success is based on pure sweat. If you are eager to succeed you should never rely on luck. **You are your own luck, no one else will grant you favors but yourself.**

Not a single dream has ever been converted into reality without sustained efforts and considerable energy in the first place. To cut it short, **energy and effort resemble a deposit sum of the full price for realization of dreams.**

Life makes an advance and becomes automatized and easier at a rapid velocity. We have arrived at the day that people require a button on their phones which will display the top chart of trending dreams when clicked. They imagine that they can flip through the dream list and casually confirm the relevant ones. A few minutes later, ta-da, the dream is activated, it is a sheer reality... Fortunately, the fruits of success don't grow on the low twigs of a tree.

If you happen to meet successful people, try asking them if they would ever trade a day of struggle from their life for bigger success? I have my grave doubts that anyone successful would ever agree on it. Actually, successful people know it down pat that **the value of achievements is measured by the amount of pain they cause.**

I know it with examples that people who were given something they didn`t earn, failed to value it.

Moreover, after a short while, they succumbed to depression because their lifetime dream was granted to them on a silver platter without the sense of joy and triumph. In actuality, "quid pro quo gifts" simply murder the interest of human just because they break a sacred rule—**everything has its price, if you want to get it you will have to pay for it.**

The top of Mount Everest means nothing if we reach it on a helicopter. Only conquered peak brings the sense of maximum triumph.

It's quite possible the sense of joy that the victory brings us, dates back to our ancestors who fought furiously with savage animals to survive. The truth is simple as that—**the best part of the victory is the struggle.**

It is momentous to never stop on what has already been achieved. Never rest on your laurels—don't be yesterday`s man. **Human is made to win continuously and beat his own records. That is what keeps us all alive**. A purpose in life is a must. In fact, **finding our purpose in life is the exact purpose of life**. It is the bond that keeps us connected with the future. Even a fleeting thought that you have already achieved everything you longed for and there is no need to conquer new heights is overly disturbing. It is a borderline death.

Let me bring a sound example of sportsmen/women. These devotees live to win and crave to repeat the joy which victory has once granted them. Their life is a continuous struggle to break more and more records.

Albeit our dreams may not be connected to any sport, we can still sense the same feeling of triumph that athletes have at the moment of victory. Life gives zillions of opportunities to outperform our yesterday`s selves and thrive for more. If we constantly keep ourselves busy with achievements, we will never sap out of the essential skills. If you happen to achieve an accomplishment, celebrate it and quickly shift to achieving the next goal.

On the other hand, failure is usually described as the disability of achieving success. But as Abraham Lincoln put it, "The best thing about the future is that it comes one day at a time." We can't take a day out of our life and classify it a mishap if the desired results were not achieved during it. Success effectively teaches us that it takes efforts and tussles to achieve it—we often get hurt before we succeed. The pain the struggle causes is not meant to signify failure. Precisely the opposite, they are believed to be the reasons that we succeed in the end. These so called "failures" resemble theorizers who whisper us through allegories and parables and can teach so much if we lead an ear to them.

The actual failure is in fact the fear of pain and loss which simply paralyzes us to take necessary actions that will change our life for the better.

Instinctively, we are predisposed to run away from pain since early childhood. Once hit we never approach to what caused us pain simply to avoid that adverse feeling. Self-protectiveness underlies our genetic code, where the pain is a threat that questions our existence. Meanwhile, in many cases the pain which may appear disturbing is meant to heal us instead of killing.

A large number of people are used to running away from difficulties that cause discomfort and pain—they simply wish to achieve everything without hustle and bustle. But think about it, isn`t it too primitive for such an advanced mechanism as human? **The tendency to feel ultimate comfort and pragmatism gradually saps us out of our unrivalled advantages as human beings—the capacity to generate valuable thoughts, the sense of ownership, the ability to control our lives and progress as individuals.**

Instead of running away from pain we need to learn how to benefit from it. In fact, **pain is the border**

where we jump out of our old skin into the person we have dreamed to be. So, be ready for severe difficulties on your path to success if you are really determined to attain your aims. Be sure that your achievements will be directly proportional to them. No effort will ever be spent in vain. Your success will be the mirror of your entire road. It may take months or even years of continuously arduous work to achieve your goal depending on how big it is. Still, bear in mind, it will finally pay off.

HOW TO SET GOALS AND ACHIEVE THEM

If your to-do list starts with "Today I build my life" there will be no time for burning the daylight.

Setting and achieving goals are very careful tasks. I have met people who didn't think long enough about the ways of achieving their goals and immediately started doing numerous things all at once. This practice resembles shooting multiple arrows at the same time and never aiming to hit the target. They walked up a blind alley from the very beginning and as a result they failed to accomplish any task that could lead to their goals. Shortly after, they lost the enthusiasm which propelled them into starting their journey. Eventually they simply gave up on their dreams.

There are certain techniques which are a must to be practiced for being able to set and achieve our goals. Firstly, it is very important to **focus on a goal at a time**, it can be anything—finding a lovely job, establishing own business, purchasing a new house, learning a foreign language, mastering favorite musical instrument, winning a medal at Olympics, becoming a popular actor/actress, getting married, becoming an exemplary parent, losing weight, traveling around the world, etc. Just draw up a list of your top 5 long term goals. Pick up the most urgent one. There are high chances that the very first goal, once achieved, will pave the road for your further goals. Let that first goal become your super task, direct your entire energy and focus toward it. Decide for yourself the deadline to convert it into reality. Jot down carefully the notes of the necessary skills that you can't do without on the way of achieving your goal. Work hard on them time and again to attain expertise. Immerse yourself into the process of learning, synthesizing and applying knowledge in practice. Meet people who have already achieved what you want to accomplish, ask them for precious piece of advice and get inspired by their sound experience. Go over your work, sharpen it, try to elaborate it on a regular basis and forget about quitting if you occasionally get tired or come across obstacles.

There is a so called "touch-move" rule in chess according to which if players happen to deliberately touch a piece during their turn, they are simply supposed to make a move with that piece. Treat your goals as chess pieces. Once touched make sure they bring the intended results.

TYPES OF SUCCESS

Types of success mainly originate from the variety of our dreams. Homo sapiens has an unlimited capacity to produce millions of thoughts. We possess a giant generator of dreams in our heads such as living a long-lasting and healthy life, having a lovely family, being financially secure, flying to the moon and back, playing on the piano like Chopin, becoming a president, a famous singer, an Olympic champion... this list is simply endless. Yet there are exceptional dreams which always stand out from the rest and are high on the list of priorities. If we try to sieve out the rather common dreams which most people have, we will have to separate them into three categories—dreams belonging to:

- personal life,
- financial life,
- social life.

In the next paragraph I mean to discuss the ways of achieving success in all the above-mentioned aspects of life.

PERSONAL LIFE

Overwhelming majority of people perceive personal life as a family life. Family is the habitat of our most sacred feelings. Almost everyone dreams to have one, i.e. a life partner and children. We need our own families to become able to share our thoughts, views, dreams, feelings and our entire life.

Statistics indicates that as a rule spectacularly successful people did marry and did have children. The sole explanation to this is that family stimulates us to work harder and achieve more, they give us moral support, inspiration to grow and prosper. On the other hand, people who have a family feel more responsible to succeed as the success of their family members has a direct link with their own achievements.

I want to place a specific emphasis on the importance of marriage just because it`s more vulnerable to failures than the relations between parents and children. We badly need a life partner—a person who will accompany us through our whole journey of life, a person who will witness our accomplishments, struggles, happy and sad moments, a person who will support and encourage us, a man/woman we can freely express our thoughts with.

Honestly, not a single person guards the secret of finding the right life partner, just because there is no secret at all. Simply put, nobody has that recipe as it varies from individual to individual. However, my happy marriage of six years taught me the exact necessities required for keeping healthy family relationships.

First and foremost, marriage should be based on love. It must be built in the atmosphere of joy, affection, respect, understanding, support, encouragement, trust, honesty, devotion, attention, care, appreciation, tolerance, patience, equality and compromise. As a rule, relations crumble because of the absence of any of the elements mentioned above. These elements are indelible parts of marriage.

Marriage should exclude criticism, complaint, doubt and lie. It`s taken for granted that every family happens to bicker, but before we start an argument with our loved ones, we better be determined to solve it in a win-win manner. It is pretty simple; all we have to do is to ensure that both parties are satisfied with the final conclusion.

Marriage should grant a space to express ourselves fully and be accepted the way we are. It should never limit our growth. Instead, marriage should support, encourage and drive us toward dramatic progress and significant accomplishments.

Marriage should not be a snap decision. The easiest way to devastate relations is to think that the partner we have chosen is not the best or the final one and/or we deserve someone better. This leads to counting the partner`s disadvantages instead of focusing on the advantages in the first place. The latter consequently grounds reasons for divorce.

Mostly people are inclined to believe that once something is broken, they can easily throw it away and replace it with a new one including marriage. In actuality, it is a misconception toward life. Human being is incapable of evading difficulties in any sphere of life, and marriage is not an exception in this case. We ought to obtain problem-solving skills to hammer out the troubles and repair the broken feelings, cure the open wounds of each other instead of giving up or trying to find the solution of the problems in someone or somewhere else.

Maintenance of healthy family relations requires continuous efforts. We can't overlook our families for a short while and hope that everything will remain the same. Family resembles all the other aspects of our life that require dedication of time to make sure we don`t miss out anything. No matter how packed our schedule is we should always devote precious time to our family, and it should always be the number one priority. After all, every single achievement loses its worth if we don`t have a family person to share the joy with. As we know our family members honor us the most and become the happiest and the proudest people with the success of ours.

FINANCIAL LIFE

The world at large wants to have a financially secure life. Finance helps us care for our life supporting, material and even some of our spiritual needs. It stands a positive stead in animating a considerable number of our dreams. In crude terms, it`s an essential means of feeling secure, confident and balanced.

Of course, there is a large number of people who were born with a silver spoon in their mouths. Yet, the biographies of the richest people in the world show that the lion's share of the millionaires and billionaires have been self-made. Most of them started from the very bottom and hardly anyone notched up success by the twist of luck.

As I was born in a family of slender means, my childhood was a real race of survival. Yet, I gave a promise to myself that as I grew up, I would work so hard that I could get out of the cycle of poverty. On my way to financial success I discovered several major reasons why the poor get poorer and the rich get richer.

The very first reason of poverty is not producing a service that the world values. Ask yourself, if you already have or need to develop skills that will bring you material profit. What can you provide to the world in exchange for money? How can you make others voluntarily take money out of their own pockets and put it in yours?

People living in reduced circumstances do various jobs which don`t bring them joy and satisfaction and then start complaining about the shortage of money. Meanwhile, all we need to do is to **make our love our business.**

Bill Gates became the richest person in the world not because he decided to do something which would bring him a huge fortune, but he loved programing and studied it with passion which later brought him cosmic benefits.

Walt Disney loved producing cartoons which made his company one of the most popular motion-picture production companies in the world.

Joanne Rowling had no idea that her "Harry Potter" fantasy series will bring her such a big fame and wealth. She followed her passion and it brought her financial success.

When we have our heart seeded in something, we do it with passion, we become an expert in

our chosen field and master it so perfectly that it automatically becomes valuable for the world thus bringing material profit. **Our love for our job is the number one guarantee for wealth.**

Debt is the second reason of poverty. Nowadays banks generously offer credits to every willing person, and we happily take them without realizing the consequences. By borrowing money, we dig ourselves into debts. Be it in the form of a loan or money which is borrowed from a friend, either way we must pay our debtors. It`s very important to be conscious that by **getting the money which is not yet earned we borrow it from our tomorrow.** This is a break of a natural law. **Service should always come first.** This is a dogma. We can't expect the world to pay us in advance. Even the food that we eat requires a significant amount of energy from us to digest before it can energize us. **Spending tomorrow`s money today promises a poorer situation tomorrow because tomorrow we will willy-nilly have to work not only for the day living but for paying back what was already borrowed.** How do we expect to get rich when our service stays behind the paycheck? As a matter of fact, getting rich or poor is a simple math. I call it the rule of **"1-2 vs. 2-1"; if you consume more than you produce you**

are either poor or on your way to poverty and vice versa—if you consume less than you produce you are either financially secure or on your way to it.

We should primarily destroy the habit of borrowing money and tighten our belts living on what we earn if we mean to escape the cycle of poverty and head to financial success. **Living without debts is the second guarantee for wealth.**

The third reason of poverty is spending money trying to gain happiness. This practice has psychological motives. I have noticed that the poorer people are the more they like to spend money. It`s because they constantly have a feeling of lack and they try to fill this gap via buying things without realizing that the more money they spend the poorer their situation gets and the deeper the hole of dearth becomes. It resembles a situation when a person pours out the water from a leaking boat without realizing that the boat is sinking not because of the water in it but because of the cracks in the first place. They spend all their money and muff the opportunity to enjoy it in their own pockets. **A real trouble occurs when a person fails to feel complete and satisfied.**

People blindly follow the universal trends of popularity as they don`t want to fall behind. We want to feel confident and significant, look metrosexual and stunning. We buy state-of-the-art cars and cutting-edge phones not because our old ones don`t work properly, or the new ones are more useful—we simply intend to astonish others and ourselves. We buy designer clothes to look glamorous and rich simply to mirror the real rich ones whose purchases don`t even constitute the 0.0001 percent of their income. These expenses cost us an empty pocket. Anyone with low financial status who wants to change his current situation should consider these purchases unnecessary as the latter are generated by the low level of self-esteem.

While poor people "sell" money to buy things rich people sell things to "buy" money.

Before purchasing anything, stop and ask yourself if it`s really worth your money. Is it truly necessary? Plan beforehand what you want to buy when you go shopping, set a list of must-have things and once you finished the planned purchase leave the store immediately to avoid getting seduced by unplanned purchases.

Developing the habit of temperance and abstention, you can build a well-grounded financial life.

Defeating the temptation of spending money is the third guarantee for wealth.

The fourth reason of poverty is the disability of saving money from the income and profiting from it. A great many of people spend all the money they earn. If someone is not capable of squirreling away at least the ten percent of his earnings he is deprived of chances to become rich one day. I thoroughly recommend saving at least the twenty percent of the monthly earnings. It may cross your mind that even the entire profit of yours is not yet enough to satisfy your daily needs, but you can prove it wrong by taking a piece of paper and a calculator and counting all your expenses during a month. It is utterly important to take into calculation even the tiny expenses such as drinking a coffee in a café ten times a month or taking a taxi. In my own practice, I can deduce that those small expenses may cost even more than all the large ones combined. You need to locate the leaking spot of your boat. There are too many unnecessary expenses which we make every day and if we cut down on them, we will see that by the end of the month we can save that twenty percent I mentioned above.

Experience has taught me that, **zero-point mounts up via the ability to save.** I distinctly remember my first-hand acquaintance with the importance of saving money, it occurred when I was eighteen years old. There was a shop that abutted my apartment house and I was in the habit of shopping stuff in it on a regular basis. One day I left the change of my purchase to the saleswoman. The latter was one of the co-owners of the family business besides being a saleslady. She was an old lady and always sounded exceptionally nice to people. Here is what she told me, "Take your change my dear, for your information we managed to establish this shop by putting aside those tiny changes." Unhesitatingly, I was too young to learn that lesson immediately but as time went by, I acquired the habit of saving money. I remember there was a period in my life when I used to work at a company remotely from home and received a decent salary, yet I didn`t even have a comfortable work desk and a chair. Simply put, I preferred saving money to making a purchase, as I tended to believe that a new desk and a chair were an unnecessary expense at that time.

Start saving today! Squirrel away the twenty percent of your earnings once you receive the salary, never put aside the money after purchases. And don`t count on that money if your monthly budget is up too early. Learn to adapt to available options.

With several months or years gone, you will have reasonable savings which will grant you a feeling of freedom. These savings should not be consumed or frozen in your bank account. They need to become an active asset and produce profit. Try finding out worthwhile investment schemes where your money can bring you profit. I don`t recommend investing in schemes that promise a drastic growth of the invested amount. In my own experience money invested in an unfamiliar market or in a business which promises a fantastic revenue becomes wasted. Try locating trustworthy sources of income. It`s very beneficial to invest in a scheme, the sphere of which is familiar to you. Moreover, if you are a master in that field, it will only do you a credit. In case you invest your money in establishing your business, it`s very important to spend enough resources on the promotion of it. Quite a few times decent businesses fail as a result of poor branding and marketing. Hustle, so that the world becomes aware of your product and improve it every single day. Soon your savings in their turn will start producing profit and you will have two sources of income. The cycle of investing the savings and the savings generated by the savings into new businesses can grow as big as you can physically manage.

The more your income gets, the bigger the percentage of savings should become. Sadly, numerous people tend to do precisely the opposite. It`s utterly difficult to keep yourself fitted in the same frame knowing you can expand but the one who looks afar never allows momentary decisions to spoil his long-term plans.

You might have heard that Warren Buffett, who is one of the richest investors in the world, still lives in a house in Omaha, Nebraska which he bought in 1958 for 31,500$. You see **financial freedom is not defined by the amount of money that we can give away. It is defined by the amount of money which we can handle.** Take his example and instead of thinking about the ways of spending your earnings focus on collecting more. **Turning our savings into actives is the fourth guarantee for wealth.**

The fifth reason of poverty is the mentality that "happiness is not in money". As a matter of fact, happiness doesn't underlie money. Money is only an option which helps us materialize some of our important dreams and thus feel happy. It helps us care for our essential needs, live in comfort, enjoy material blessings of the world, travel and increase our views. It also gives us freedom to become a better person by helping the people we love and providing comfort to them.

People who are inclined to believe that money is something demonic, that it blurs human`s spirituality, have zero chances to escape the cycle of grinding poverty. Additionally, this mentality is illogical because people, who use money to satisfy negative ambitions and cause damage, can easily do it without money as well. Money is only an option and just like anything else it can be used both in positive and negative ways and it can't "spoil" us as long as we don`t spoil ourselves.

Money is not an enemy to people but rather a support. Don't we value the food on our table, the roof above our heads, the clothes keeping us warm? All that I mentioned were provided to us in the exchange of money. In fact, money is not just the paper which we exchange for buying and selling things. **Money the measurement unit of the service which we render to the world.** Once we start hating money, we will start hating our own service, our deeds and consequently ourselves. **If our jobs make us feel deliriously happy, we**

should as well be happy with the value it has in its financial equivalent.

I made an observation according to which the poorer people are the more they hate money, yet the most intriguing part is that a great many of them hate not so much money itself but the fact that it is in others` pockets. An interesting paradox, isn't it? Money is evil to them as long as it doesn`t belong to them, but sadly, the antagonistic approach from the very beginning and envy they have for others shuts the doors that could lead to their financial welfare.

Desire to get rich is the fifth guarantee for wealth.

Summing up this paragraph, it can be inferred that financial well-being requires doing what we love in the first place, stay out of debts, abstain from spending recklessly, save and profit from our savings and have a burning desire to get rich.

SOCIAL LIFE

Human is a social being. We simply can't deny the importance of other people in our life. One of the greatest human accomplishments is the creation of civilization which exists solely through human relationships. In actual fact, we need other people for millions of reasons starting from viable support to spiritual needs. If we were alone in the world, we would never even discover our strengths and significance. The latter become unveiled only in the event we compare our abilities with the abilities of others. **If we isolate ourselves from the rest of the world and lead a secluded life, we would no longer thrive to win, progress and surpass our own selves.**

Each and every person wants to be accepted by the world. It`s the social life that helps us gain love, support, fame, respect and reputation. These are key elements for human`s self-esteem.

Achieving success in social life requires a pleasant personality in the first place, i.e. the characteristics which will be meticulously described in the next chapter of this book. Soon you are going to discover the inner qualities a person needs to have for achieving tremendous success in all aspects of life.

CHAPTER 2

SUCCESS COMES FROM WITHIN

...and in darkness you discovered you can shine.

In the previous chapter I expanded upon the understanding of true success and failure, the essence of dreaming, setting goals, planning and acting which are key factors for achieving success. The latter pave the path to desired results. Nevertheless, they only make the one side of success, i.e. they form a skit played on the stage only, it is what the world notices. In fact, there is mountainous work done behind the curtains which no one ever sees but you. This vast work resembles the functions our inner organs do for us which are unseen, yet so vital. A human is simply incapable of surviving with only one of them being dysfunctional.

To unlock the full capture of success we simply need to study the "anatomy" of those organs which are mentioned below:

- *belief*

- *self-confidence*
- *focus and concentration*
- *discipline*
- *persistence and patience*
- *counting on yourself*
- *courage to take risks and timely decision making*
- *keeping promises and taking responsibilities*
- *enthusiasm and motivation*
- *optimism and winning attitude*
- *laughter*
- *imagination and creativity*
- *curiosity and personal growth*
- *adaptation to changes*
- *time management and life balancing*
- *accepting failures and moving forward without regret*
- *gratitude*
- *kindness, tolerance, compassion, generosity*
- *humility*
- *speaking beautifully*
- *saying "no"*
- *coping with others` opinions and forgiveness*
- *getting comfortable with uncertainty*
- *overcoming the fear of death*

People having all these organs functioning in harmony look lively and full of zeal. They have their unique magnetism, and everyone likes to follow them. They are true leaders, rare to meet but if you ever happen to meet one you will easily distinguish him/her.

True success is born through the sum of all the above-mentioned qualities and to become successful in every field of life we need to discuss each of these qualities and the ways we can develop them in ourselves and eventually profit from them.

BELIEF

Dreamers are many, believers are few;
the latter make dreams come true.

It`s not a coincidence that all religions exist through belief. With belief we recognize and accept the things which our five senses are incapable of perceiving.

Still, expending upon belief, I don`t necessarily mean the religious belief. Belief is a universal phenomenon and can be applied to literally anything. All of us have beliefs even if we are blind about them. Beliefs are essential parts of our existence.

Beliefs can be both constructive and destructive. Through the constructive form of belief people think they can get from life whatever they want, as life is wonderful and full of opportunities to succeed. On the other hand, there are people who tend to believe that they are incapable of changing their lives, as the world is cruel and unsafe. This is a sound example of the destructive form of belief which constantly causes people to fail.

The way belief works is simple. Firstly, generate a thought in mind—be it a positive or a negative one. Secondly, spice it up with belief. In the aftermath, you will have either an amazingly cooked meal or a poison served for you.

Science has countless evidences of the enormous impact beliefs have on our lives. Medical history is full of innumerable proofs that placebos (a medicine or procedure prescribed for the psychological benefit to the patient rather than for any physiological effect) had profound effect on patients` recovery. Whereas noceboes (detrimental effects on health produced by psychological or psychosomatic factors such as negative expectations of treatment or prognosis) contributed to patients` deterioration of state. The nub of the matter is **every single thought energized with belief can either heal or harm us depending on its nature.**

To succeed in life, our beliefs should be linked only to positive thoughts. In my experience, belief played a significant role in paving a path to success. I had a firm decision to convert my dreams into reality, I worked backbreakingly and truly believed that one day I will have my orders from the universe delivered. That strong belief guided me through uncountable difficulties, and almost everyone I knew thought I was an empty dreamer. But finally, I achieved what my mind believed was possible for me.

There are certain techniques which can contribute to the development of strong belief in you. The latter include **visualization, affirmation** and **prayer**.

The way visualization works is relatively simple—all you need to do is to visualize the picture of your desire and imagine as if it`s already happening to you.

This practice should be done alone in a quiet corner, so that nothing would destruct your attention for you to submerge into another reality. You may turn on some calm background music. Close your eyes and free your mind from everything, relax and concentrate on the focal point of your dream. Imagine it in detail, try involving all your senses. Let all your cells get comfortable with the feeling that you already possess it. Enjoy your presence in the picture of your dream, make it feel like reality. Once you visualize your dream in your mind, you are already one step closer to it. Envision can become more realistic if you seek the evidences of your dream in real life. For example, if you dream to own a beautiful house visit one which is on sale, even if you can't yet afford it. Enter the rooms and imagine them yours, think about the ways you would decorate them, find your special favorite place, and enjoy that wonderful feeling of being there. Believe me, that feeling will accompany you even upon leaving the house. For the next session of visualization, you will have something to add from your memory as well. Latterly, your determination to fulfill your goal and the belief that you can achieve it will undoubtedly become stronger.

Before becoming a celebrated actor, Jim Carrey took out his checkbook and wrote a check to himself for ten million dollars. In the memo field he wrote, "For acting services rendered." He closely guarded this check and kept it in his wallet as a constant reminder of his goal and finally, years later, he made his ten million dollars from the movie "Dumb and Dumber". This is an amazing example how visualization helps us deepen the belief we have, stay motivated and focused on our goals.

There is a fancy tradition in my family which my husband and I developed years ago. We always keep a bottle of champagne in our house. As you know champagne is a symbol of celebration. Having one at home subconsciously makes us find a reason for opening it—a reason for celebration. And the reasons don`t let us wait long; almost twice a month we replace the bottle with a new one as we celebrate significant achievements. Surprisingly our achievements become bigger and bigger by each time. This is how the "magical" bottle of champagne urges us to succeed more. We believe that having one at hand, we will definitely find a good reason for opening it soon.

By means of affirmations, a person can keep his mind focused on his goals. It is overly essential to use affirmations which are solely positive. I started doing it years ago in front of mirror. At first, I sounded weak and unsure. But gradually my voice gained certainty and became loud, I even had times when I found myself screaming with tearful eyes from the energy that my words brought me. Create your own affirmations which suit you best and let them be simple. Try expressing your exact goals and repeat them several times a day. Alternatively, you can jot them down and stick on the walls in front of your bed, so that your goals become the very first and last things you see and think about before and after sleep.

Prayer in its turn is proved to have an enormously positive impact on people since day one. Prayer switches our mind to a trance where we communicate with God. If you don`t have a religion, you can call your prayer a communication with the Universe. Your prayer should necessarily be honest and rise from the deep recess of your soul. As a matter of fact, upon praying people become certain and calm as if they received a guarantee that everything is meant to move to the right direction.

Using the above-mentioned techniques on a regular basis helped me develop ultimate belief in myself and my chosen destiny. This makes me sure you can benefit from them as well. To transform your dreams into reality and let the magic happen, you need to first of all deeply believe in your dreams!

SELF-CONFIDENCE

No one can stand on the way of someone who knows where he is going and is doing it with confidence.

Self-confidence is a wonderful quality that is developed solely through experience. The competence of doing things on the subconscious level builds the highest form of self-confidence.

We simply can't gain self-confidence if we are deprived of sufficient knowledge and experience in what we do. Constant repetition of specific actions that are aimed to success make us a master in that field thus boosting our self-confidence.

Self-confidence is prevalent among all the successful people in the world and all of them have gained that character through working arduously and mastering their area of expertise. This feeling is like a flame which keeps us warm when we run into unfamiliar situations in life. It grants us peace and tranquility even in case of adversities. Simply because we know we can rely on ourselves, on our strengths and abilities. Self-confidence is the smooth background music of our life and it can brighten any situation. It`s our satisfied attitude towards ourselves, the personal mark for our own accomplishments, our pride. It is a list comprising multiple mega-achievements recorded on our behalf with exact dates of all our victories.

It`s taken for granted, that there are people who competently pretend self-confidence to look attractive and successful or open some doors in their life. However, this practice is deprived of authenticity as it`s a form of pseudo-confidence, i.e. a simulation. "Self-confidence" with no background of experience resembles a mirage of a fountain in the desert. It may appear alluring from afar but once you reach it to quench your thirst, it simply vanishes in the air. In this book I am expanding upon the true self-confidence gained via efforts and practice, i.e. the ultimate belief in personal power which is proven and acknowledged as it comes from within and resonates positive energy from inside.

Becoming a self-confident individual is not a piece of cake. In order to develop it I recommend spending significant hours a day on the acquisition of the skills which can lead to huge success. Once you become a master in your area, your self-confidence will boost automatically.

FOCUS AND CONCENTRATION

A mind that is constantly busy with how to achieve success won`t fail.

Focus is the hub of our thoughts and activities. It comes from the Latin word 'focus' which in 17th century meant "hearth, fireplace." I can't say exactly how the word focus evolved from "hearth" into a "spotlight", but if we look closely, we may spot a close link between them. Focus is the place where the fire burns, it is where the energy is concentrated, the hub we gaze at.

When we focus on a task, we gradually discover multiple details about it. Analysis helps us understand all the segments of the task and take a full control of it, just like looking at the task through microscope. These details are not visible for people who work in a superficial manner. These individuals don`t realize that God is in the details.

Focus contributes to filtering out the unnecessary information from mind so that we

become able to stream all the energy into a single direction.

There is a thought-provoking technique that shows how focus works. Close your eyes, think up a color, and try imagining it vividly. Now open your eyes and look around. Your mind will automatically start filtering that color from everything you see around.

Unfortunately, most people can't even get down to doing work for 2 consecutive hours with no interruption, let alone focusing on tasks which demand years of continuous commitment in order to reap the fruits. These people have a huge number of thoughts spinning around in their heads and find it very difficult to pick one and stick to it.

There are numerous recognized methods to advance focus and concentration, including: finding a focal point and staring at it, thinking exceptionally about what you see, and examining it in detail. If you come to realize that all of a sudden, your mind gets busy with a different thought, get rid of it and continue gazing at the point.

I have found my own simple method of enhancing focus and it comes quite handy. I turn on two different melodies simultaneously and force myself to focus on listening only to one of them.

At early stages, becoming concentrated is rather challenging, as you will start realizing how many random thoughts cross your mind within a minute. Yet, through practice you will soon manage to gain full control over your concentration, hence profiting from it.

More often than not, if the task we work on brings us enough joy and makes us excited about its results, we tend to become concentrated more easily. On the other hand, if the process doesn`t keep us engaged, it might be resulted from the lack of love toward it. Therefore, the questions that rose in the beginning of the first chapter require urgent answers. When there is joy in what we do, coupled with full concentration we are unquestionably on the way to success.

Lack of concentration might also be caused by physiological reasons, such as: missing much-needed sleep or malnutrition or even skipping physical exercises which support the proper functionality of our brain. These factors are not of lesser importance, so I recommend devoting rapt attention to your sleep hygiene, physical activities and diet as well.

DISCIPLINE

*I don`t compete with anyone; others are too lazy to
run my race.*

Real life is not a sole competition, it has millions of
"finish lines". People, who are not willing to work
hard on their dreams, tend to have an excuse—too
many people are competing for success in the field
they chose to succeed. In actual fact, it`s not true,
i.e. they don`t even bother to participate in any of
those competitions. Basically, in those millions of
races only an overly few disciplined people
participate for the reward which is success. The rest
remain in the shoes of observers without realizing
that instead of stargazing they could possibly
become "stars" too.

Discipline is believed to be one of the most
fundamental elements in the construction of
success. It is activated at the very moment we want
to halt or procrastinate the assignment that was
scheduled to be performed on that day for the
realization of goals. Sometimes we might not be in

the mood of performing the tasks that were planned beforehand, yet a person with rigid discipline, will avoid an evil chance of seizing on an excuse to halt it. Discipline resembles an inner boss who has no mercy on weaknesses, monitors everything carefully all the time and makes sure the task meets the deadline. It develops punctuality in a person, defies explanations such as being bored, tired, upset, etc. Moreover, it forces us to put everything aside and get the work done.

After I launched my company most of the people who knew me were not even surprised at my achievement. They simply observed the level of discipline I worked with for years, so my accomplishment was just an inevitable result of the progress. I tussled for seven consecutive years in a hectic schedule that included working twelve to sixteen hours a day before I could start my business. I took it on the chin, as I never complained to myself for aiming so high. My daily routine was so packed with so much work that very little time was left for other activities. Whereas, I knew perfectly well that I was doing it all for my today`s self, and now I do realize that the efforts I took were worth my current achievements. I don`t necessarily mean that people should forget about everything else and devote themselves entirely to accomplishing a single task—not at all. As a matter of fact, this practice has detrimental effects and I am not an exception in this case. The frantic schedule of mine resulted in health problems, which gladly I managed to overcome before it would become too late for me. The nub of the matter is, **discipline simply does the job we consider boring.** Abraham Lincoln put it, "Discipline is choosing between what you want now and what you want most." What is more important for you—today`s short term pleasures or tomorrow`s profound achievements that can bring you peace and stress-free life?

Truly, it`s not so easy to become a disciplined person. The only way is trying to force yourself to continue doing the things you have to do to harvest an ample crop. Skip saying, "I need a rest" and "that is too much to handle", even when you run out of energy. I know that most of all you deserve success. Look farther than today`s short-term needs, as **your deepest dreams carry the most meaningful needs which are a must to be satisfied**, and discipline will keep you concentrated on them. The best part is that once you teach yourself to be more productive, disciplined behavior will become a habit and gradually a part of your character, i.e. you will no longer need to force yourself to do something as it will be natural to do.

Try learning about the billionaire routine. Albeit fabulously rich, most of them still wake up early at six o`clock in the morning. They go to work first and leave the workplace last. These work-related habits were shaped by strict discipline and demands that successful people had toward themselves, and they are now simply a part of their character.

Remember, **the Universe never grants gifts for doing nothing, but she always replies to our gifts (efforts) sent to her and her feedback is so generous**! Whatever we give returns to us in an enormous amount, just like the seeds we plant return in abundance.

PERSISTENCE AND PATIENCE

Patience is the shield of your dreams, persistence is your sword; never put them down.

Persistence is an astounding power that doesn`t allow us to give up. It lives in the athlete that crosses the finish line, the climber that conquers the summit of Mount Everest, the teacher that builds strong individuals in the class, the musician that creates a blessing for our ears, the mother that raises her kids alone, and the toddler that keeps on falling until finally learns to walk. Persistence lives in you and me if we decide to never give up on success.

I know dozens of cases when people came across the very first obstacles on their road to success and hastily gave up. They simply lacked enough fortitude to stand on their own and demand their right for success. Quitting and crossing the dreams off their dream list soon left them with a futile page and a heart filled with disappointment.

Success should be a burning desire, a life-supporting value that we can't do without. Think about it, **if we**

70

knew that achieving success is the only way out to stay alive, would we retreat so easily, or would we at all? I have my doubts.

I vividly remember a mishap that occurred about ten years ago when I was swimming in the sea. It was a cloudy evening when all of a sudden, I realized that I had swum too far, where the water was wavy, and the shore was hardly seen. I pulled myself together, concentrated all the strength in my arms and started swimming back even though the stubborn waves were blowing me to the opposite direction. Reaching the shore was a vital need for me. I had absolutely no choice but to be persistent enough to reach ashore; otherwise I would simply drown. Gladly, I coped with it. This accident taught me a lot about the power of persistence. **Any adversity, be it a life-threatening or a minor one, offers us two choices—giving up or overcoming it**. If you think you can easily manage without a dream you have little chances to fight for it and make it come true. **Treat your goals as elements without which your life would be questioned, and persistence will guide you on the way to your goals.**

Persistent people are unshakable, as nothing can stop them from doing what they have already decided to do. If you have never heard of Nick

Vujicic, a man born with no limbs that lives a full life and motivates others to do the same, I wholeheartedly recommend doing some research on him and listening to his amazing speeches. He is a sheer example of a man with iron persistence.

Patience is the powerful ability to live fully in peace while waiting for something significant to come around. It`s the most effective and beautiful way of waiting. Patience keeps us in motion towards our goal while it is still away from us and always finds a way to entertain us by keeping us busy at the time, we are climbing our "Everest". Patience helps us to find joy in the present time while we are heading to the future. It`s a plentiful evidence of self-control and shows how much will power we have. It doesn`t bow to time and changes but lives according to its own rules.

As a matter of fact, people don`t set long-term goals, because they simply lack enough patience. They can't wait years even for their most desirable dreams.

Take the bright example of Thomas Edison. We know that he invented the incandescent electric light bulb. But, can you believe that he failed ten thousand times before perfecting it? He had a priori infinite patience and iron persistence.

I believe, one can hardly find anyone who skipped watching the movie or reading the autobiography book of Chris Gardner called "Pursuit of Happyness". He was a homeless man with a toddler son trying to make both ends meet. He could hardly survive through grave problems and difficulties but finally succeeded in becoming a multi-millionaire investor. He followed his dreams and through persistence, patience and hard work changed his whole life becoming an inspiration for our era.

Confucius said, "It does not matter how slowly you go as long as you don`t stop." So, whether you make a catwalk, or a marathon run to success, just don't give up in the middle please.

To see the dawn, we must first survive the night!

COUNTING ON YOURSELF

Real maturity begins at the very moment we start counting on our own selves. This is the freedom of choice to decide how we want to live and what we need to do for living boldly.

A large number of people simply don`t rely on themselves. They are not the ones who guide their life. They follow someone`s advice or example, anything or anyone but never their own selves. Instinctively, they pursue a person they can trust, someone who will have enough mercy to guide them and help them build their life. These people live in an autopilot mode, always searching for solutions everywhere except in themselves and taking whatever the life will throw at them.

This situation gently reminds me of an old joke. A poor man was constantly praying to God to send him money. But God stood silent. Time elapsed, and the man started to complain that God was simply ignoring him. At that very moment he heard God who said, "Just do something, at least buy a lottery ticket."

On the other hand, resilient people who tend to take total control of their life and fully count on themselves always attain greatness. They know that the shortest way to success lies in their own selves, simply because **no one else is more eager to transform your dreams into reality than you yourself**. These individuals are not inclined to wait for favorable opportunities and charities from luck; their mind is set on reaching success on their own.

The funny paradox is that **people who take their own steps to notch up spectacular success are prone to receive the gifts of luck more often; success starts walking toward them in its turn to accelerate the awarded meeting.**

COURAGE TO TAKE RISKS AND TIMELY DECISION MAKING

I risk because I care about the consequences.

Quite a few times people need to take educated risks without which there will be no progress. But sadly, most often we realize the weight of the opportunities that could change our life completely after the right time becomes a past and the favorable circumstances are gone. What was required from us was only to analyze the situation smartly and to act. By failing to run risks when they are required, we become doomed to live our lives picturing what could possibly happen had we the courage to take the right steps on time.

Mostly, people are afraid of shouldering responsibility for an action which involves even one percent likelihood of failure. So, what if we fail? Hardly any failure can have fatal consequences. Yet, the reward of the risk taken on time that brought success is always tangible!

Another reason of procrastination is considering yourself unprepared. Some people prepare so long that eventually miss out the time to participate in the "show". The signs of their beautiful future are everywhere, and they carry so many opportunities, but they turn into unrealized and expired potential as we don`t make noise on their arrival. They say, "One day I will get higher education, I will start doing the job that I love, I will quit smoking, I will go to gym... but today is not that day". To me this sounds like **"I will change my navigator to success after I waste enough time on driving to failures".** They even fail to dimly realize the sound fact that **no matter how many times you multiply zero the outcome will always remain zero.**

Our self-confidence, determination and analytical skills come quite handy for taking the initiative and acting on time instead of goldbricking to act. The right time is always now! It`s the only time we have at hand. As an old Chinese proverb puts it, "The best time to plant a tree was 20 years ago. The second-best time is now." So, dare act now!

KEEPING PROMISES AND TAKING RESPONSIBILITIES

Leading roles are occupied by people who are willing to keep promises and shoulder more responsibilities.

The ability of keeping promises and shouldering responsibilities for our actions is a distinct sign of maturity. Caring about the consequences of our words and deeds makes us reliable and trustworthy for others. I bet there is not a single person who is eager to deal with someone that is not as good as their words or isn't willing to take responsibility for personal deeds.

A word that is uttered must be brought into action by all means, if we fail to honor our own words, we prove we don`t have control on ourselves. In the aftermath, we shouldn't expect others to believe us and our words. If we want people to hold us in respect, we need to respect ourselves first. Importantly, we need to have reasonable grounds to earn our own respect. The ability of never going back on promises is a large-scale investment in that business.

The willingness to shoulder more responsibilities implies readiness for further growth and success in our life because the amount of responsibilities we handle is directly proportional to our level of growth. Responsibilities symbolize our acceptance of providing more service to the world. While on the subject, we already know that the one who gives more receives more.

Some people tend to believe that genuine freedom is having no responsibilities at all. But it`s a mere misconception. If we didn`t have any responsibilities it would mean we wouldn`t have any role in life, nothing would be dependent from us, i.e. we simply wouldn`t add any value into this world. Having no responsibilities at all is equal to non-existence. Hate it or love it, all of us have our own liabilities and duties. **The difference between a successful person and a loser is that the first does his responsibilities eagerly and the other avoids them.**

By accepting more responsibilities, we welcome positive changes in our life.

If you plan to move up a career ladder don`t ask the superior for it, build your growth by simply immersing yourself into the job you do. Try doing much more than you are obliged to, show interest and initiative and stay at least one hour more in the office. Be an eager beaver. Your superior will undoubtedly notice your willingness to shoulder more responsibilities and will ask you to accept an offer of a better-paid position once they start counting on you.

If you want to raise your kids as strong individuals, try devoting more time to them, burn the midnight oil studying new methods of positively affecting your children and use them practically.

If you are not happy with your grades at university spend more time on the subjects which need to be studied more, take additional classes for them, find and practice ways which can contribute to the increase of your concentration and memory.

You can solve multiple problems easily in every aspect of life via this technique; **just because you are willing to give more you are promised to get more.**

Responsibilities are the other side of the medal of success. A great many of people are inclined to think once they become successful, they will no longer have reasons to worry as everything achievable would already be achieved. I hate to say it, but it is a gross misconception. If you think that becoming successful is a daunting task, then get ready for a more challenging phase, which is the maintenance of success! The achieved success is not yet the "finish line". Moreover, **our milestones solely signify the "start" that leads to a completely new phase of life—a phase where rapt attention is required**. On one hand, we deserve to enjoy our earned rest but on the other hand, we should always keep our duties in control. If we lose the control and miss out our duties for a short while or do them perfunctory, we will become obliged to restart everything from the beginning as everything will simply vanish into thin air. That`s why it is so important to monitor every aspect of life, for what is the joy in receiving a trophy if it is taken the next minute? Instead of shirking responsibilities, try shouldering them as a natural part of life, and you will not regret that success was not permanent.

ENTHUSIASM AND MOTIVATION

I often watch the trailer of "Future" so I can play in
"Present" excellently.

Enthusiasm and motivation are born of the why-s which evaluate our actions. The more significant the why-s the bigger they grow.

These qualities are very typical to visionary people. When an idea crosses their mind, they envision the end before putting the start into action. The greater that final result looks like the brighter enthusiasm sparkles in their brain.

Enthusiasm and motivation are the children of love, belief, imagination and hope. But just like any newborn baby they need care and attention. They are the gasoline we fill ourselves with to reach the desired destination. Love and passion toward the work we do bear enthusiasm and motivate us from within. Feeding them on belief, imagination and hope will gradually turn them into an inseparable part of our existence.

I vividly remember how my husband mentioned once that many of the gyms he visited had special mirrors which reflected people with larger muscles. This practice motivated the visitors to work harder on gaining the desired shape, as they imagined that one day the true mirror would reflect them in a better shape too. After witnessing this, an idea crossed his mind according to which **everyone should have an inner mirror which will reflect them in the combination of the desired future,** and it can help to stay motivated and work on success with more enthusiasm.

Immensely enthusiastic people are easily recognizable, they are like candles which spread hope and joy around them. They have a contractible drive of delightful life and speak so energetically that everyone becomes eager to listen.

There are many productive ways to develop enthusiasm and motivation externally as well, particularly through reading books about success, listening to the lectures and interviews of successful people, watching motivational movies and finding a mentor.

During the darkest periods in my life when I happened to doubt myself and even have fears of possible failures, a few hours a day I used to listen to the motivational speeches of truly inspirational people like TD Jakes, Les Brown, Eric Thomas, Jim Carrey, Tony Robbins, Jordan Belfort... There are really so many people who deeply inspired me! For me they resembled a sign "Never surrender!" They helped me become courageous and stay focused on my goals and I acknowledge a debt of huge gratitude to them for my success.

I cherish the hope that following these methods you can as well keep yourself highly motivated and strongly focused on success. **Become the person that doesn`t bow to failures, but worships success and gets inspired by it even if it is still afar.** Let enthusiasm make your struggles and failures remembered with smile when you reach to the pitch.

OPTIMISM AND WINNING ATTITUDE

If you don`t see the beauty in your life try healing your vision.

Optimism is a state of mind which helps us to stay highly focused on positive thoughts. Every single person wants to see the bright side of life, but many don`t know how. These people are stuck in the rut of negative thinking. It`s like a bog that pulls them down lower and lower until they finally get drowned. The irony is that such people have a dichotomic approach towards the optimistic ones; they tend to believe that positive thinkers don`t take their life seriously, i.e. they fail to take full responsibility of it, with anything they own being granted them by merciful twist of luck. This belief contains monumental errors. **Optimistic people take life so seriously that they don`t let it go in vain and in pain.** They get the best of it and never stress out because of the things which are wrong or might go wrong. They work on solving problematic issues instead of letting them control their lives. Whereas negative people do exactly the opposite.

Negativity is a deadly enemy of success. It blocks every road that leads to success and opens the gates of misfortune, misery and poverty. Worrying and overthinking about negative things which haven`t occurred yet or things that have a slim chance to happen is like waving them from afar and calling them, "Hey I am here, notice me, come over here!"

It's a tough challenge to switch attention to the positive side of life; I know it from my personal experience. I was in the habit of worrying on a regular basis about things that might go wrong. In the aftermath, I felt like I was gradually becoming a magnet for misfortune. Later on, I learnt about the law of attraction according to which whatever we think we become. I firmly decided to get rid of the pernicious habit of thinking negatively. It took me several years to train my mind. Consequently, I found out a very interesting antidote against overthinking, worrying and agonizing myself; **the best way to avoid the worst is to get ready for it**. **Focus on the best but be ready for the worst. The bones of fear are buried under every unresolved problem**. Solve the potential problems before they knock on your door together with their adverse consequences. **When you set your mind on a mode where you are psychologically prepared for everything you automatically stop worrying.** You accept the life with all its shades and don`t panic even when a mishap occurs—you just face it and show it that you are not made of glass but iron.

Indeed, there are so many things beyond our control, yet we are always in control of our own behavior, accepting the failures and problems in a way they can`t hurt us. After all, **the worst thing that can happen in our life is the end of it, and so long we are alive we should live, and we should enjoy the entire process of living!** The Bible says, "Consider the ravens: for they neither sow nor reap; which neither have storehouse nor barn; and God feedeth them: how much more are ye better than the fowls? And which of you with taking thought can add to his stature one cubit? If ye then be not able to do that thing which is least, why take ye thought for the rest?" (King James Version, Luke 12:24-26)

Winning attitude is a very potent weapon if we mean to fight for our dreams. Before engaging in a battle, we ought to envision the victory, otherwise we are destined to failure.

The easiest way to develop a winning attitude is to celebrate all our achievements including the

smallest ones. Every trophy we win should be distinguished and praised. Get your heart used to the feeling of victory so you can seek successful outcomes everywhere.

LAUGHTER

When we go to the cinema, we simply pick a movie to watch, then we learn about its genre which automatically sets us in the relevant mood as we enter the cinema hall. We don`t prepare ourselves to let out a laughter when we go to watch a thriller. Yet, knowing that it is a comedy we enter the hall already smiling.

I brought this example on purpose as it has a direct link with our perception of life. When a person perceives his life to be more of a comedy genre, he becomes ready to laugh even at his own failures. I am sure everyone has seen videos of fail compilations. These videos may include disturbingly dangerous or even life-threatening failures, yet they make us laugh, because they are categorized under the comedy genre.

Laughter saves people from depression, panic and boredom. Moreover, **the ability of laughing at our own mistakes and failures makes dramatic alterations in the construction of our life scenario.** Laughing at own mistakes is probably the most generous performance of self-criticism, the expression of the highest level of sense of humor.

I tended to believe a person needs serious reasons to laugh before I came to know my husband. Naturally, he is a great comedian. Everybody adores him for his sense of humor and positive energy. No matter where he goes, he makes people laugh and feel happy. His style is simple—he never waits others to entertain him but rushes first to change the atmosphere via his positive energy and humor. He simply creates a positive environment through kind words and funny jokes. He conclusively proved to me that it`s possible to laugh even at the smallest things—I really mean it. Good sense of humor and laughter are essential ingredients of happy life. We don`t need to wait for Kevin Hart`s shows, we can literally find fun in every single day and laugh so hilariously that people around start joining us.

We know full well that those who laugh a lot are happy. Importantly, it`s a proven fact that laughter brings happiness. In fact, laughter releases endorphins that are similar with drugs such as morphine. The latter arouse the feelings of euphoria. **Laughter and happiness can both be the cause and the consequence of each other**, it is like the endless argument whether chicken or egg came first.

Humor can open the heaviest doors in the world. It unites people and creates a positive atmosphere. People who possess a high sense of humor always achieve everything they want. Even the toughest person is incapable of restraining his laughter hearing something ridiculously funny. Laughter melts the tension and feud, boredom and exhaustion.

Many people use this radiant instrument in almost every situation. They turn a family quarrel, a serious job interview into a fun and in the aftermath, they attain positive solutions and results. Moreover, they can even turn an illness into a recovery.

Years ago, I read an article about Norman Cousins, a journalist who was diagnosed with a serious life-threatening disease in 1964 called Ankylosing Spondylitis. The doctors told him he had the merest chance to survive. Later, he discovered that both his disease and the medication were depleting his body of vitamin C. Hence, he produced a brilliant solution to his complicated problem—he left the hospital and refused to take any medications. He started receiving massive injections of vitamin C and spent most of his time watching comedies that made him laugh (we all know that laughter releases vitamin C).

In the aftermath, he lived till 1990, 26 years more than what the doctors predicted. Isn`t it a miracle?

I strongly recommend taking your daily dose of laughter and generally treating life with humor. We can't foresee the length of our existence, but we can surely make our life more pleasurable through laughter and positive mood.

IMAGINATION AND CREATIVITY

Imagination is the ability to form mental images. It`s a unique attribute that distinguishes a human being from other types of creatures. The ability to recreate forms that already exist into something completely different is just fascinating. By combining them in an original way we bake a completely different cake, and this is how imagination works.

The world is changing at a rapid velocity due to imagination and creativity. Everything we see around has first been an idea in someone`s mind—a result of imagination. Ever since electricity was invented the number of inventions exceeded the number of all human inventions made before. After technology entered into our lives, it never ceases to amaze us with more and more inventions emerging every single day.

Some people believe they have a dearth of imagination to create something beautiful in their life, but it`s not true. It`s like insisting they don`t have the right hemisphere in their brain. Every human being has imagination and creativity, but just like any other human function they grow through constant practice and repetition.

It is overly essential to realize that imagination and creativity are usually shaded in an eclipse when a person tends to have negative thoughts and attitude toward life. Consequently, imagination needs a free space and a pleasant environment to grow otherwise it will stay dysfunctional.

I highly recommend taking the example of children if you mean to boost your imagination. Look how differently they perceive the world. Childish views are neither standard nor familiar ways for us to perceive the life. We laugh when kids take everything into their mouth or wear the bucket for toys on their head or call a chicken a crocodile (that was me). In actuality, they have a bright imagination and see wider possibilities of using things than we do. To become able to change our viewpoints and notice everything differently we must first accept the fact that there are possibilities of different realities just like knowing that blue is blue and yellow is yellow but blended together they are red.

It`s a breath-taking experience and endless fun to apply imagination in everyday life—it can produce comprehensive solutions to dozens of problems in a creative way, making our lives easier. Who knows, it may even add your name in the hall of fame if you work on developing it and bring the fruits of your imagination into life.

CURIOSITY AND PERSONAL GROWTH

Life is wonderful as long as we wonder.

In the beginning of our life we had millions of unanswered questions about how things are made in the world. Our childhood was a non-stop process of discovery composed by the answers to what-s, why-s and how-s. We wondered about everything new to us. But, as time elapsed, we gradually quit asking questions mistakenly thinking that we already know everything that is necessary.

Every day humanity makes ingenious inventions and startling discoveries which are the direct results of curiosity and wondering ability. Both inventions and discoveries were achieved because some grown-up people did not lose the ability to wonder and grow. If truth be told, before these inventions emerged, we couldn`t even guess they were there waiting to come up, i.e. we can't even imagine how many wonders are still well hidden from our eyes!

Curiosity propels humanity into progress, it boosts our growth which is the most indispensable element of a healthy life. It is the most effective remedy against the illness of boredom.

Every human being is born with an ultimate potential of growth. Growth has no limits, i.e. it is as big as the universe or the multiverse. Our little brains have a colossal capacity for new information and knowledge. They are so immense that can pack the whole Milky Way inside. We the humans are the most perfect creatures on the planet Earth, and we are so blessed to possess the ability of thinking, analyzing and developing our knowledge.

Humanity has numerous brilliant minds to its name including Albert Einstein, Isaac Newton, Charles Darwin, Fibonacci, Galileo Galilei, Hipparchus, Aristotle, Confucius, Leonardo Da Vinci... This list is endless. When we hear their names, we take a deep breath, feeling inspired and proud of representing the same race. In fact, no one can be them, yet we all can leave a powerful heritage by being ourselves and developing our unique capabilities, just like they all did.

Our potential is just unlimited. Each of us has individual abilities. If we zoom out and try looking at things from an eagle eye perspective, we will see that notwithstanding our differences we are all one product on earth—a product that can think and create.

Growth of the human should be an ongoing process. We should always challenge ourselves to learn more and welcome the unknown into our lives. Schools and universities are not the punchlines of our growth. There is always a room for more knowledge.

People who read voraciously and acquire new skills never lose the ability to feel young at any age because the youth has a strong bond with the process of learning new things.

If you try conducting a research, you will come to realize that many famous people rose to fame at an old age including Anna Mary Robertson Moses, who began her prolific painting career at 78. In 2006 one of her paintings was sold for 1.2 million dollars. Gladys Burrill ran a Marathon at the age of 92 and earned the Guinness Book of World Records as the oldest female to complete a marathon. John Glenn went to space at age 77 and became the oldest person to travel in space. Noah Webster completed his "American Dictionary of the English Language" at age 66. In fact, this list seems to have no end. Isn`t it stunning to see these people`s enthusiasm in learning and growth and desire to reach greatness even at an old age?

As a matter of fact, we can't become old if we don`t stop growing. Age does not determine our life.

If you feel like your life got deprived of a key element as a result of which it`s gradually becoming boring and monotonous, just take a look around and perceive everything the way you did back in your childhood—try looking at things through the prism of wonder and curiosity. Never stop asking the fundamental questions that evoke new ideas, such as what, why, how. I encourage you to deepen your knowledge and acquire new expertise. Start reading books with titles that intrigue you, discover new knowledge. Then practice the acquired skills on a regular basis if you intend to advance them. Wonder and curiosity can bring back the magic to our lives and maybe even come up with something new for humanity which will change the world for the better.

ADAPTATION TO CHANGES

Human is the strongest amphibian that can live both in peace and in trouble.

Adaptation is the process of fitting to an unfamiliar environment and circumstances. It plays a key role in success. Accepting and participating in a cardinally changing life full of unusual and difficult stages, keeps us attached to the reality.

Everyone happened to get into a tight spot when the situation was not the way they wanted it to be—unsuitable, uncomfortable and tricky. Can you recall the way you acted back then? Did you cope with the reality quickly enough and took measures to improve the situation or simply ran from it hoping it would change by itself?

I vividly remember reading an informative article about a psychological reaction called "fight-or-flight" which was first described by American physiologist Walter Cannon in 1920s. The term "fight-or-flight" represents the choices of people when faced with danger—they either fight or flee, i.e. there are people who try solving the problem when they get into a hot water, whereas others run away in the face of a trouble. The "flight" group of people panic and let the circumstances take control over the situation when they come across obstacles. To escape the cycle of unpleasant situations, we should eliminate the burdens gathered on our way. The latter are usually the consequences of our mistakes—either our done wrong or undone right deeds. Anyway, if we try to analyze the situation, we come to know that **what looks like a problem is actually the handle which we hold while moving up the stairs toward our better selves**. Problems give us a golden opportunity to fix the wrong things in our life. They hide an unlimited amount of potential that can alleviate and make our lives way better.

Unfortunately, many people don`t cope with problems easily. Fixing problems requires a dynamic approach to them, i.e. the ability to see them both under microscope and telescope to define their substance. We need to analyze them thoroughly to find their causes and solve them, just like doctors assign medicine after examining the patient and finding out the cause of the illness.

I want you to believe that you are in full control of your life. **You are not a victim, but a warrior**. Expect the best from life and act for it. **Don`t feel satisfied with your result if you just didn't lose but aim at winning every battle on your way to a lucrative life.**

TIME MANAGEMENT AND LIFE BALANCING

Time is the most wonderful gift granted to us since our birth. Undeniably, it is the greatest of all our resources.

Time management is the ability of sorting out the right priorities on everything in our life. Nowadays every single person expresses discontent because of time deficiency. Yet the truth is, humanity has always had twenty-four hours a day. It has neither increased nor decreased at least during the past two millenniums. Importantly, almost everything is automated nowadays which makes our lives easier and surely saves a lot of time. The knotty problem is that most people don`t know how to identify priorities right. We constantly see people rushing up to manage multiple things all at once but at the end of the day they still have a great many of planned tasks unaccomplished. In fact, **being busy is of secondary importance—all that matters, is what we are busy with.** There are so many unnecessary things to keep ourselves busy with nowadays that we can hardly draw a line between what is meaningful and what is useless. We could undoubtedly manage our lives better without that one-hour phone call, the addictive TV programs and soap operas, the practice to follow every update on social media, the lazy extra hour sleep after the alarm clock, etc. If we summarize the amount of time, we spend on non-productive things every day, at the end of the year it might make one third of the entire year if not more! **Instead of following others and spending useless hours you can work on yourself and carve out a person who would be followed by others.**

People who know full well how to manage their time, have enough of it for job, family, personal growth, social life, physical activities and rest. They have no reasons for regret as they manage their time consciously. Fabulously successful people have always kept that balance between the above-mentioned important parts of life. Just imagine, if Thomas Edison always had time for his mother despite his hectic schedule, how dare we complain and justify ourselves for having no time to spend with our families? Instead of frittering the gasoline of our life on the roads that take us nowhere, wouldn`t it be better to plan and spend it wisely? After all, **before wasting our precious hours, we better consider that one day we will expire our last one**... So, let`s start using our time meaningfully!

Even though focus on achieving a goal is utterly important for success, it`s also necessary to make sure not to forget about other essential aspects of life. Our life consists of family, job, social relations, personal growth, entertainment, healthcare and rest. If we only focus on job alone, we might lose everything else. It`s like having many plants and watering only one of them. We can't get back to the others after the first one starts producing the harvest. The rest of the plants will dry out in the meantime if we don`t care about them as well. As a result, some people succeed in pursuing a glittering career, yet they fail to participate in the most important family events, miss the childhood of their children and the chance to be a good parent and a husband/wife. Time flies, and the opportunities are gone. Sadly, we can't replay the same day again.

To live a great life, we must be a servant and a master at the same time; work hard for tomorrow and reward ourselves for yesterday. This is how we should keep the balance in our life and most importantly be fully present now!

ACCEPTING FAILURES AND MOVING FORWARD WITHOUT REGRET

I owe my success to my failures;
without them I wouldn`t be so focused on success.

The road to spectacular success is always full of formidable obstacles. No matter how thoroughly we plan it, we always risk failing somewhere. In fact, failures are not crucial, i.e. they never mean we should stop where we paused. During these breaks we need to take a breath, try finding out the reason something went wrong, sum up our thoughts, fix the issues and head forward. **Failures are opportunities to perfect our journey. They are as important as success itself; we recognize ourselves merely after being tested by both.** They build up a forceful character and strength and make success more triumphant when attained. Just like medical pills which are unpleasant to taste but surely cure us, **failures help to increase our**

immune system against inevitable situations in life.

Wise people never treat failures as the end of the road, they never dishearten because they know perfectly well that **the only way to become a victim is to feel like a victim**. They respond to tough challenges of life and make failures part of their progress and success—they transcend their yesterday`s selves. Life becomes more predictable and simpler for people who follow these methods.

Regret comes from the realization of our failures and mistakes. It`s the mother of misery. Those who feed on profound regret are forever chained to their past. Through regret we merely confirm that the current situation is miserable and somewhere in the past it was much better or could be better if we took decent steps in the past. **Accepting failures does not yet mean we should regret for what we have (not) done. It is the capacity to diagnose an acute disease after which the cure follows**. On the other hand, regret is what keeps our focus on what can no longer be changed, it worsens the current situation and makes life unbearable. Regret turns the present into past, depriving people of any chance of having promising tomorrows. Living in the past is like replaying the same movie again and again hoping fervently that it will have a different ending. Regret disarms us and binds us hands and feet. It causes both physical and psychological illnesses.

Every day up to seventy billion cells die in our bodies but we continue to live. **It merely takes us to block some negative memories and deaden destructive feelings such as regret to be able to start living in full.**

No matter what happens in our life we should always keep the focus on our present and future. Let the visions of the future be brighter and clearer than the mirages of the past. Instead of replaying the scenes of failures in your head throw them into the recycle bin as soon as you draw the necessary lessons from them.

Our everyday life is what we can fully control, therefore **missing today from the radar promises new failures and regrets.** Time undergoes a sea change at every moment. It never waits for us to catch up, it`s downright savage toward lethargic individuals. So instead of feeling a twinge of bitter regret, we better accept our failures, rise and move forward to embark on hair-raising adventures.

GRATITUDE

The key of gratitude matches to the door lock of happiness...

Have you ever felt the ultimate power of a sincere gratitude for your deeds? It stimulates us to do even more, doesn't it? A genuine "THANK YOU" has a touch of magic that brightens our day. Every single person loves the feeling of being properly appreciated and becomes willing to do even more for the one who has applauded their efforts.

As a matter of fact, a person satisfied with others is keen on not mentioning it considering it an unnecessary sentimentality. To make things worse, quite frequently we don`t even realize the value of good others do for us. On the other hand, even the slightest ground of dissatisfaction rises the devil in us. We give freedom to spiteful complaints and bitter criticism thinking naively that this practice is meant to fix the problems. I have niggling doubts if this mentality is actually preset in human genetics, yet we are so prone to getting irritated and expressing anger that we often don't realize the harm it causes others and ourselves. Criticism of itself carries so much negativity that it immediately shuts the doors to others who start protecting themselves from the harassment of negative energy. And it`s conclusively useless to hope that people will shift into doing things right as a result of complaints and criticism.

As soon as I discovered this pattern, I decided to apply it on practice. The company I worked in, had a network operating center which was not working very proactively. I repeatedly complained to them about failing to give the necessary technical support on time. Once I read about the magical effects of gratitude, and I thought about the ways to use it at work. I had a group conversation with the technical support team. Firstly, I apologized for my frequent complaints about the results they produced and mentioned that it was very egoistic of me to ignore their diligent attitude toward the work they were doing for the benefit of the company. I thanked them genuinely for everything they had done and were ready to do, I voiced my gratitude for their passionate devotion and punctuality and for their patience with me. These words were not just uttered to them for proving the magical effect of gratitude— they were honest, and I meant every word I voiced.

They thanked me back for my support. One of the technical engineers became so inspired by my words, that he devised a slogan and wrote on it, "One Team, One Dream, Guardian NOC Team." It was truly an amazing experience to see their productivity triple within a short while.

Since then I altered my conduct and decided to never again complain. Instead, I set my mind on pointing out solely the good sides. Today, whenever I want to hammer out an issue that is brought by others, I first thank them and compliment on being so great at fixing it—it's a magic as it solves the problem and leaves me with no more reasons to feel dissatisfied.

The rule of gratitude is universal. We have millions of reasons to be thankful for in our lives. Every single day of life is a blessing. Thanking itself is outstandingly beautiful. It`s the expression of mind showing that something is totally right. Don`t ignore the power of genuine "thank you"; it lights up all the stars inside everyone. Thank as often as possible. It will not only spread gleams of light upon others but will spark a flickering flame inside you as well. Thank the universe for being so generous toward you. Instead of counting the things you lack, try having a grateful heart that notices every tiny good around you and in yourself. After all, **we don`t need to wait until we lose everything including our life to become aware enough to notice and appreciate the life itself**.

The Bible says, "For whosoever hath, to him shall be given, and he shall have more abundance: but whosoever hath not, from him shall be taken away even that he hath." (Matthew 13:12)

This wonderfully empirical truth can be related to every good thing in life, among which is gratitude. Thank and you will be given more, because the Universe is so generous!

KINDNESS, TOLERANCE, COMPASSION, GENEROSITY

Only dividing we multiply.

You might think that this paragraph is written for giving a moral lesson and at some point, it will be right, because it`s beyond the realms of possibility to attain spectacular success not having high morals. It`s virtually unknown how morality became an integral part of humanity, i.e. whether we were born with it or simply obtained it through the experience of generations. Yet, everybody agrees that if humans did not have it, the life on earth would immediately vanish. We exist because we do carry morals—they are the guardians of our life, the borders that keep evil away from kindness. Be it a beautiful present gifted to the human race by God or something man-made, we all recognize it.

Still, there are individuals who tend to believe that a great number of successful people reached fame without having high morals. In that case, I advise them asking themselves, if it would be natural for rivers not to water the trees alongside, the sun not to warm and the roses not to smell. No one can consider himself successful if his achievements bring joy only to himself. **We just can't light a candle and expect it to shine solely for us**. Just like this, we simply can't become successful without having kindness, tolerance, compassion and generosity in our hearts.

I can`t emphasize enough the importance of kindness one needs have to be able to find happiness in his life. Kindness is a major element for feeling well-balanced, harmonic with the surrounding world, peaceful and natural. In other words, kindness helps us to feel human.

There are three forms of kindness: **kindness in return of kindness, kindness in return of nothing, kindness in return of evil**. The first and the foremost common practice of kindness is responding to someone`s charitable deeds in the same manner.

The second type implies good intentions to the surrounding world as a person is simply ready to help others in return of nothing.

There was a video that recently went viral on internet about an act of kindness which demonstrates the first and the second types of kindness. An illegal immigrant from Cameroon climbed a building in Paris to save a boy who was about to fall from a balcony. He could just be one of the observers but instead he put his life at risk and saved the child. Later that day the president of France met him personally and granted him French citizenship. Kindness solved his dire problem. Of course, when he followed the command of his pure kind heart, he was unaware of the reward, but the truth is people most often appreciate kindness and help you back.

The highest form of kindness is the last one mentioned above. It is when a person remains kind even when the rest of the world thinks that the opposite would just be fair. This form of kindness is born from infinite wisdom and very few people on earth possess it. Generally, people are inclined to reply in the same manner. In fact, **a person knows he is truly free when his feelings stay calm even in case of bitter adversaries.**

Mahatma Gandhi put it, "An eye for an eye only ends up making the whole world blind." Gandhi`s life was a pure expression of the highest form of kindness through which he could unite a quarter of the world`s population. I highly recommend reading his biography and studying his character meticulously.

He is a bright example of a genuinely kind person. And before you decide to ever hurt someone know, **you measure the pain your sword can cause by first experiencing it on yourself, thus hurting yourself in the first place.**

Tolerance is an uncanny ability to endure everything we dislike or disagree with. It creates a complete harmony between each other and everything else surrounding us. In crude terms, acceptance of all forms of existence is a distinct sign of infinite wisdom.

The universe is widely diverse, yet not a single thing is designed the way to contradict anything. It is a tight union of markedly different forms of existence with their unique functions and roles—they are all chained in harmony. Tolerance creates an endless communicating circle of healing energy which surrounds the universe not letting it explode.

People with tolerance are not prone to anger or hatred, i.e. they accept and respect others` right to live and express themselves the way they want. They fully comprehend the fact that the world would vanish into thin air without substantial difference. They grow up through acceptance of realities which are out of their orbit.

Just ask yourself, is it possible for a human being to survive with all organs carrying out one and the same function? The tiny factories that we call bodies exist solely through harmony and unison of the multiple functions of our organs.

The world`s population will soon reach eight billion. This brings out the question—how on earth is this possible to expect everyone to have the same interests, opinions and views on life or think that our views are the best ones? What is right for you and me can be wrong for someone else, while tolerance helps us cope with bewildering varieties and forms of existence.

The biggest compelling evidence of intolerance were the World Wars and the genocides of the last century which shook the earth. Hopefully humanity learnt a lesson from these fundamentally dreadful mistakes and will never ever repeat them.

Everyone can practice tolerance toward others— every time you find a plausible reason for disagreement try overcoming your ego, putting yourself in the shoes of the opposite person. Try seeing the world from the contrary perspective. You will be utterly amazed to find out a completely different reality that probably would be acceptable to you be you in it.

Compassion is the ability to pity and feel concerned about problems and misfortunes of others. It`s a forcing function that extends a helping hand to others. With all our virtuous deeds summarized, the picture wouldn`t be complete if we still lack compassion. A person without compassion resembles an empty gift box. Yet the ones with it, undoubtedly have the stamp of God on their hearts.

Generosity is an uncommon ability of voluntarily sharing whatever we have. Generous people never worry that generosity will deprive them of things. They simply enjoy the process of giving tremendously. They made a personal discovery according to which **the giver is the true getter**. For how much joy their generous acts bring them! Happiness is a strange phenomenon that doesn`t comply with any scientific explanation—the more you share the more is left. We become deliriously happy when we offer our help to people who badly need it... Is it a coincidence that the word 'enjoy' originally meant "to give joy"? So, be generous toward others, learn to share your best, for only dividing we multiply...

These moral qualities guarantee a lovely successful life, a pleasing and amicable personality that attracts other people like a lighthouse for the lost ships. Following them grants an inner peace, i.e. a feeling which brightens life and feeds your soul with an endless bliss.

HUMILITY

Failure taught me to stay persistent, success challenged me to stay humble.

Another beautiful attribute, which is an indispensable part of success, is humility. It is what establishes a stringent limit on human ego so that it neither explodes nor rises. Instead, humility brings human ego down to earth even when his fame has reached the sky.

In fact, no one loves supercilious people. They are personas non grata. A great number of people who managed to attain power and become fabulously successful feel so proud of themselves that gradually that feeling turns into something hideously ugly. These people start to consider themselves the hub of the universe. They desperately want everyone to adore them but despite the magnitude of their power and success, people tend to avoid them. In the aftermath, they breed hatred around them instead of the aura of awesome respect. Their success is just a fad, a glimpse of time, as no one will stand next to them once they fail.

On the other hand, people who stay humble despite their widespread fame and success happen to raise their names even higher. They gain overwhelming love and considerable respect, simply becoming a sound pattern to follow.

Some people mistakenly believe that the primary reason they remain humble is that they don`t realize how immense their fame is. As a matter of fact, these people simply realize how small their achievements are compared to what still waits to be achieved. Despite the substantial number of their accomplishments these people willingly accept that they are just ordinary earthy individuals like everyone else. Modest people never separate themselves from the rest of the humanity. They respect and sympathize with others. They never ridicule people who fall behind or are less successful. Instead they try to help them notch up success as well.

For gaining tremendous success we need to learn to keep ourselves down to earth and simple by holding back from vainglory and vaunt. This practice will only add a touch of additional beauty to our personality.

SPEAKING BEAUTIFULLY

*There is no way to measure the impact of kind words,
yet we can witness the magic they do by changing the
perception of our minds.*

The power of words was revealed to humanity since day one. Numerous ancient tales and legends tell us about people who used words to work miracles. As a matter of fact, words can wage or put a halt to gore wars, heal or cause illnesses, bring joy or sadness, hope or disappointment, create love or hatred, construct or destruct—they have an ultimate power of doing literally anything. Words which are converted into a speech are born in our minds, i.e. they are the stems of the plants, the roots of which are grown in our minds. Words help our strongest and influential thoughts to emerge. If you direct an assiduous attention to someone`s speech, you will soon discover his character and personality, feelings and emotions, dreams and goals, hopes and fears, past and future. Words cogently express our personality traits; therefore, it is so important to think carefully every time we are about to say something. If our words are meant to cause destruction, it is better to not speak at all. Instead, we better analyze the root of such thoughts, i.e. the reasons they were born in our mind. We simply ought to find the source and work tirelessly on altering our mindset.

Powerful words which arouse deep emotions are easily memorized; words of encouragement, love, belief, joy, etc. I vividly remember the time I was leaving school, and my literature teacher entering our classroom, standing right in front of me, and saying, "I came with a sole purpose to tell Ani to never quit writing and bid a farewell to all of you." Twelve years later, I must confess, I often recalled these words as they left a significant impact on me. Maybe it`s one of the reasons I always knew I would write a book. These powerful words acted as an expectation for me, encouragement and belief—I truly feel so obliged to her.

Speaking about the power of words, I can`t bypass the depressing truth that nowadays the usage of swearing words in our daily language is taken for granted. People don`t even feel uncomfortable with the inappropriate language that carries negative meanings and destruction. People need to comprehend the fact that the presence of swearing words in the speech doesn't augment the importance of the meaning. Moreover, pejorative words are utterly harmful for health. The latter may cause severe illnesses which is a proven fact. On the other hand, eloquent words born of kindness tend to have a healing impact on people.

Our libraries are teeming with dictionaries that contain an inordinate amount of beautiful words, which faded into oblivion. Instead of repeating the same lexicon over and over again, it would be better to learn at least a new word every day or try replacing a commonly used word with a synonym. We form an opinion about smartness and character of someone by the way they talk in the first place. So, enriching the daily vocabulary is never a waste of time.

Words have a marked tendency to materialize. This is how positive affirmations work. Words that we utter quite often put down roots in our unconsciousness, i.e. they become part of our existence and our reality. A person addicted to complaining about his life merely confirms that life is not going to change for him, whereas the one preaching kindness to others, plants the seeds of warm-heartedness in their hearts including in his own. Our words have a profound significance, so we`d better handle those weapons wisely—mouth needs to be tightly regulated as every word a person utters has his signature below it. This cautious approach makes us monitor every single word we express—it helps us to entirely exclude the elements of negativity.

Eloquent and impassioned speech can turn every conversation into joy. There are several techniques to be used during conversations. The latter guide us to healthy relations with people who surround us.

Conversations are meant to arouse positive mood and attitude—nobody would mind listening to someone who radiates happiness and smile. By the same token, not a single individual would consent to listening to tedious and mind-numbing complaints.

Every conversation can bring the desired results if we initiate it with questions and compliments that aim at the participant(s). As a matter of fact, people love attention toward their personality, i.e. they want to be noticed, interested in, and simply cared about. Knowing this on your own example you can apply it in your interactions with others and you will be pleasantly surprised how simple sentences like "How have you spent your weekend?", "Is your mother feeling better today?", or sincere "You look amazing!" turn people into sweethearts.

Conversations should never include criticism toward the participant(s) of the conversation nor toward anyone else not present in it. Criticism is a "stop" sign on the road to building strong relations. It implies a negative attitude and simply forces the participant(s) to keep distance from you instead of just opening their heart. Criticism toward people who are not engaged in the conversation just implies that a person may betray them at any moment and do the same against them. On the other hand, there are cases when people start criticizing others harshly and you turn that bitter criticism into something positive, saying, "You might be right that he is talkative, yet I should say that he gives an amazing piece of advice." This tactic stresses up several key features of yours—you are trustworthy, positive and generous. Simply put, someone they want to have around.

Conversations that include animated discussions of a problem should head to finding solutions and not focusing on the problem itself. A person who is even minded and optimistic would always suggest multiple ways of solving knotty problems.

These techniques are utterly useful for creating a sympathetic and harmonic contact with others. Importantly, we will make them a part of our positive character if we practice them on a regular basis. Hence automatically becoming a person who everyone cherishes and wants to have around.

SAYING "NO"

Saying "no" instead of "yes" and "yes" instead of "no" is the real cause of chaos.

A great number of people find it pretty challenging to say "no" to others when it comes to doing a favor or listening to what they are not eager to. Even kindly polite people who are willing to help others aren`t supposed to do everything they are asked for. We have our uniquely own perception of everything and only we can decide on things that are bad for us and sacrifices we are ready to take in order to favor someone. Sacrifice itself is a voluntary form of hurting own self. People who are in the habit of making sacrifices willy-nilly develop a pernicious habit of self-destruction. In the aftermath, they gradually lose control over their own will. Their acts for the welfare of others not only fail to bring happiness to them but start causing frustration and anger toward others as well as their own selves. They lose love and respect for themselves for they become unable to simply say "no" to doing things that hurt them.

By exhausting ourselves thoroughly we will never ever be able to make the world a better place. The nub of the matter is, acts of kindness are natural forms of human deeds and they don`t require neither a force nor pain to be vitalized. **Doing everything for others and not caring for your own needs is not a sign of generosity but rather a conspicuous lack of self-love. Generosity should first be applied on the closest person one can ever have—his/her own self.** There is an old saying: "What's sauce for the goose is sauce for the gander." Our deeds for the benefit of others and our own selves should not be in contrast but rather in harmony.

I highly encourage you to firstly care for your own needs because it will give you enough power to care for others with no loss being required from your side.

And secondly, I do advise to run away from people who willingly accept your sacrifices as they prove themselves uncaring about you because of their inflated ego.

The same goes to listening to negative stories of others. Moreover, I highly recommended skipping to listen to negative people. Say "no" to them. Stay away from their distinctly negative energy. That energy is contagious and wears out everyone who inhales the toxic—you don't need the venom they spit around. These people resemble black holes that absorb energy. To put it bluntly, trying to help negative people is a total waste of time, as they don't have any free space in their mind for anything new. They are like rooms with no doors or windows to walk in—no entrance to deliver the point. The Bible says, "Give not that which is holy unto the dogs, neither cast ye your pearls before swine, lest they trample them under their feet, and turn again and rend you." (Matthew 7:6)

So, I advise you to stop mercilessly sacrificing yourself for the benefit of others and to stay away from negative thinkers as far as possible. You will do yourself a huge favor by simply saying "no" when it is strictly necessary. You have the right to do it!

COPING WITH OTHERS`
OPINIONS AND FORGIVENESS

The one who judges someone`s sins, sins too.

People may lack anything but never opinions. Our opinions are the very means by means of which we filter the reality—they are uncountable. It`s quite logical that each and every person has millions of them as they are the outcome of mind, the model of thinking and perceiving everything around.

The problem occurs when people try spreading their personal opinions on somebody else. People might believe they know the best and their particular opinion is the most objective one, forgetting that in our three-dimensional world no one can really have an objective opinion. We all see different views from different locations through different filters.

People are prone to be influenced by the opinions of others. Usually the most influential ones come from the people that are close to us—the ones who we tend to listen to. Generally, their intentions are meant to guide us to the "right" direction. Yet, they can cause us severe pain when despite respect and love we cherish to them we are still unwilling to follow their examples which look horribly wrong to us.

Each of us should follow his own dreams, goals, plans, ideals, and thoughts. We need to leave our own footprints on earth and not copy anyone else`s. **We have the right of our own autonomy!**

In fact, almost all fabulously successful people have received harsh criticism on their way to spectacular success. These people were often deemed wrong, odd, detached and even silly. Let`s take for example the lives of Walt Disney, Oprah Winfrey and Ellen DeGeneres. These outstandingly fortunate individuals heard so much severe reprimand in their life that if they gave a way to any of the comments on their name, their lives would never be so inspiring. Walt Disney was fired by a newspaper editor because he "lacked imagination and had no good ideas", but later he managed to establish one of the best-known motion-picture production companies in the world. Oprah Winfrey got laid off from her position of TV anchor because she was allegedly considered "unfit for television", which led her to launch her own television network. Ellen DeGeneres, being the pioneer among celebrities to announce her sexual orientation received tons of stringent criticism to her name. Yet, the criticism didn`t hinder her from starting her own talk show and becoming one of the well-known comedians in USA.

Sadly, criticism is a usual phenomenon and the more successful a person becomes the more envy is spread around him. Additionally, it's quite probable that whatever a person has done wrong in the past will emerge to the surface and become a topic of heated discussions. People better be ready for it, because success distinguishes them from the rest of the world.

It is beyond the realms of possibility to earn everyone's love, acceptance and respect. Suffice it to say, everyone has their own reasons for hating us with those reasons sometimes having nothing to do with our mistakes. Whatever people see in others is possibly something they carry in themselves. Their judgment and criticism usually reflect what was unrealized by their own selves.

There is an old story about two monks which is a bright example of this truth. The monks were crossing a river when suddenly they noticed a woman that was also about to cross it but was deadly afraid. The junior monk picked up the woman and carried her across the river. Later, the young monk said, "As monks, we are not permitted to touch a woman, so how could you carry that woman on your shoulders?" The older monk answered, "I set her down on the other side of the river in a minute, while you are still carrying her."

The negative opinions of critics and sceptics live with them, become their reality and spoil their own lives. They usually burn the daylight extensively discussing others, maliciously gossiping, blackmailing and trying to cake others with dirt. Yet Mahatma Gandhi said, "Nobody can hurt me without my permission." I have my own method of combating criticism and the easiest way to cope with it is to be apathetic to it and persevere.

If your road is second to none don`t be weakened by criticism or hurled insults from naysayers because they will follow like a raindrop. If you aim high and intend to reach your goals, be sure that there will be numerous people with free opinions to discourage you or to mislead you. It will be overly difficult to stay out of the torrent of negativity which will spread around your name. Still, all you can do is to continue living in your own way and keeping yourself focused on success. You don`t have to prove anything to anyone or approve yourself.

Guard your aura from attacks, **neutralize the negative energy flow toward you by responding to it with positivity.** It takes enormous efforts to reach the level where nothing and no one can disturb your peace or cripple your ego. Believe you me, it is really possible. Remember **the oak does not change the form of its branches when the wind blows, it continues to live the way it wants.**

The ability to forgive is nothing but a superpower. Forgiveness is the act of pardoning an offender. According to etymology, the word 'forgive' originates from the Latin word 'perdonare', meaning "to give completely, without reservation". Indeed, by **forgiving we give the best of us.** It is the highest form of generosity. Basically, forgiveness is not meant so much to favor others, as in the first place to favor our own selves for our own sake. It doesn`t let anger and frustration poise our own lives. It closes the door to revenge. The ones who forgive have a priority against those who build plans of revenge. They continue to live and let the pain go instead of focusing on it further. Such people normally have stronger health and live longer.
If we are not in control of altering the thoughts and attitudes of others toward us, we can at least change

our own, and the most optimal way to do it is to achieve it through forgiveness.

It is also overly vital to forgive ourselves for our own mistakes. A person constantly blaming himself for the wrongdoings committed in the past is attempting suicide every single day by crumbling himself into pieces.

It`s downright fine to fully realize personal wrongdoings and accept them—every human being makes mistakes that cause regret as a consequence. Anyway, I dare to say that it`s not healthy to blame yourself and recall mistakes throughout your entire life. All we can do is to forgive ourselves and to learn a lesson from the mistakes so that we never repeat them in the future. What is already done can`t be undone, no matter how many times we try revisiting the scene in our memory.

In my experience, blaming yourself causes a severe self-destruction and makes you appear horrific from any perspective. If you happen to experience that feeling now, please, follow my advice, remove that onerous burden that you have been carrying on your shoulders so far. Forgive and accept yourself the way you are because **you are the person with whom you are destined to spend the rest of your life, so let yourself relish it**. You ought to know that **you**

are a wonderfully beautiful creature who deserves to live in pure happiness and lasting peace. You are worthy to be loved by your own self!

GETTING COMFORTABLE WITH UNCERTAINTY

Tomorrow is an empty tape until we record on it whatever we wish.

While many people seek transparency in everything, I dare to say that the best attribute of life is the sense of uncertainty about the future. Imagine if we knew the forthcoming events of tomorrow, ten years later or our last day. Would it be interesting to live further? I have my doubts about it. Knowing the events beforehand would undoubtedly spoil the whole intrigue of life. We would simply lose interest in living, i.e. we would not feel joy when good things occur, would not hope for good when bad things come out, would not feel anything, just because everything would already be known. Simply put, our biography movie would already be released before we could write the script of it.

As a matter of fact, numerous people believe in destiny, i.e. our lives had already been predetermined before we were even born. Hence, the uncertainty of the future brings fear for tomorrow and makes them heavily dependent upon circumstances. Consequently, their lives become controlled by anything and anyone except themselves. Surprisingly, in the 21st century there are still people who consult fortune tellers to learn something about their future in order to be better prepared. Yet, the truth of the matter is that everyone is the creator of their own past, present and future.

By nature, we are given the freedom of choice, which is an inseparable part of our fundamental rights—it gives us zillions of options to carve life out. **Freedom of choice is the value without which life would have no value**. It just makes us who we were, are and will become. Instead of pinning the blame on stars, fortune or destiny, we just need to realize that **it is us, and only us who are in charge of our own lives.**

Every successful person knows it for certain. Importantly, every leader on earth follows that prime pattern throughout his life. They always trust and rely on themselves and know perfectly well their next step irrespective of any situation. Even though, they can`t predict the unpredictable, they never panic nor retreat in case of adversity. Instead, they control their feelings and actions and never let the flow take them wherever it wants.

The competence to control ourselves and the circumstances where we happen to be, makes the uncertainty of the future seem secure. In other words, **the only way to live comfortably with the uncertainty of the future is to accept that we have power on our own thoughts, feelings and actions in any situation.**

OVERCOMING THE FEAR OF DEATH

The deepest fear of a human being is undoubtedly the fear of death. Every grown-up person has experienced moments of deliberation on death. Even the slightest idea that we will cease to exist one day leaves an unpleasant feeling and reminds us about our temporality. This is undeniable, no matter how successful, powerful and healthy we are, either way, all of us will be gone one day.

With no scheme to decrease the credit of how significant life is, I should say, that death is not as disconsolate as we might often consider. Basically, death is the logical consequence of our life. Coming to life people mistakenly believe that they managed to curb the life, yet the truth is that humans only borrowed it for a while. So, one day we will willy-nilly have to free up our space on earth for someone else to occupy. **All that we own is time—our time to enjoy our presence in full.**

In fact, if we analyze the picture it would become clear—**we fear not so much of death itself but**

rather of failing to live decently within the scope of our lifetime. This is the primary reason, people who managed to live purposefully and follow their dreams simply accept the inevitability of death with a calm heart. Therefore, it`s overly essential for each of us to establish our lifetime mission and to fulfill life with it. Our lives are short when compared to the eternity, whereas long enough for us to comprehend its meaning and succeed by living all our dreams. Consequently, we ought to get busy with living instead of crumbling our life by dint of the idea of inescapable death.

INTEGRITY

In this book we learned that success is born in our thoughts in the first place by obtaining the form of a dream, and finally strong wish and planning make it a goal which demands thorough repeated actions to turn into reality.

We also learned about the inner qualities necessary for success, which are belief, self-confidence, focus and concentration, discipline, persistence and patience, counting on yourself, courage to take risks and timely decision making, keeping promises and taking responsibilities, enthusiasm and motivation, optimism and winning attitude, laughter, imagination and creativity, curiosity and personal growth, adaptation to changes, time management and life balancing, accepting failures and moving forward without regret, gratitude, kindness, tolerance, compassion, generosity, humility, speaking beautifully, saying "no", coping with others` opinions and forgiveness, getting comfortable with uncertainty and overcoming the fear of death.

Success as such becomes unattainable if even one of these aspects is missing. To cut it short, success is the alliance of all these qualities, with each of them being indispensably vital to succeed in life. None of them has a secondary importance, so every single element counts massive and permanent success.

With integrity we orchestrate the above discussed "instruments" for success in such a way that they start producing harmony. Integrity is the sole source of balance in life. It is the indefatigable energy that unites various functions and creates an endless communication among them by dint of which the whole "body" of success prospers and grows.

It might appear overly challenging to activate and harmonize all these elements at an early stage as it requires an alteration of the whole functionality of our brain but gradually you will start doing it by default without expending considerable efforts.

By constantly developing and applying all these instruments in your life you will be destined to succeed massively, i.e. your every single day will have triumphant dawns and dusks, and eventually you will come to realize all the sacred dreams living in your every single cell all these years!

CONCLUSION

Live the way the stages of your life are written down on pages and the pages of your life are played on stages.

Upon arriving at the conclusion of this book, I feel a blessed relief to be able to share with you the brilliant rules by which the universe coordinates our beautiful planet.

We learned about the key elements a person needs to obtain and develop to feel deliriously happy and become utterly successful. These amazing elements are so natural and harmonious with the entire universe that, living a wonderful life does not really require any force or arduous efforts. We just badly need to fully participate in life and use the unflagging energy we are empowered with in a constructive way.

I do hope this book will grant you enough strength to fight fiercely for your vivid dreams, achieve your well-deserved success and transform your life into bliss. I share this wonderful ticket, that I formed piece by piece, and ask you to save it in your heart.

Now it belongs to you. Let it accompany you on your miraculous journey to your all-inclusive life...

I have been thinking a lot about the reasons that propel human beings into searching an outside support for feeling genuinely happy and satisfied with life, and the answer came to me in the form of an Eastern legend. We are simply not looking into the right direction, i.e. our eyes desperately search for the solution in the outside world while the treasures are hidden in ourselves. The legend is about the gods who decided to create the world. In the aftermath, they created everything including human. Finally, they created the truth. The gods intensely discussed the location of the truth to be placed in, so that humans could not find it easily. After a great many of conflicting and mixed opinions the oldest and the wisest of the gods put it, "We will hide the truth in human`s heart and he will look for it in the entire universe without a slight doubt that he carries it in himself."

Bear it in mind, that a human being is born in a perfectly full combination and whatever we are looking for has already been gifted to us at birth. Epictetus said, "The essence of philosophy is that a man should so live that his happiness shall depend as little as possible on external things."

Thank the Universe that gave the most valuable gift one can ever imagine—the life. Let us use that gift to the full extent every single moment until it expires... No matter how formidable the obstacles will be on our path, life will always remain million more times preferable than the idea of nonexistence. Importantly, life just can`t imagine itself without you! Our willingness to live and make it outstanding is the only reason that the world goes around and never gets exhausted.

Isn`t it a pleasure to be alive! We came and will go from the life show like evanescent visitors. So why should we complicate the partaking we were bestowed with by things which look so petty in the picture of eternity!

Instead of asking for "fish" learn how "to fish" by yourself because you have all the instruments in yourself to notch up the desired results. So "fish" your happiness! You are the originator of true miracles! You are the author of your life book, so make it a masterpiece! And don`t be afraid to get lost in life. That will never happen because you are as important as the universe. Your existence is as valuable as every single ring in the huge chain that creates the infinity.

Following the truths described here I know full well you will attain what is yours—something your mind has already achieved. I believe in you, and I will be the very first person to applaud your achievements... Finishing this book, I wish you a mesmerizing life! Let it be as epic as the odyssey of the old sun that, reminiscing his journey from the very first raw light of the dawn till the last luminous fire string of the dusk, knows he lived his best!

www.anishahverdyan.com
contact@anishahverdyan.com

ANI SHAHVERDYAN

Ticket to All-Inclusive Life

Your Life-Changing Guidebook

Non-fiction, Self-Help, Personal Growth

10217451R00088

Made in the USA
Monee, IL
25 August 2019